GOD OWNS IT ALL

FINDING **CONTENTMENT** AND **CONFIDENCE** IN YOUR FINANCES

RON BLUE

with MICHAEL BLUE

 **ORCHARD** ALLIANCE   *in partnership with*   RON BLUE INSTITUTE

Published by Ron Blue Institute © 2016 Ron Blue Institute, LLC, and the Ron Blue Institute for Financial Planning, LLC

ISBN 978-0-9998673-6-5 • Item 005774869

Dewey decimal classification: 332.024
Subject headings: PERSONAL FINANCE / HOUSEHOLD BUDGETS / SAVING AND INVESTMENT

We want to give special thanks to Thrivent Financial, the founding sponsor of the Ron Blue Institute, for granting permission to use the *struggling, surviving, stable, secure,* and *surplus* terminology on the sequential-investing chart depicted in this Bible study.

To order additional copies of this resource, visit www.faithandfinance.org

Ron Blue Institute, LLC – 1886 W 50th Street, Marion, IN 46953

Printed in the United States of America

Ron Blue Institute, Marion, Indiana

contents

About the Authors

RON BLUE

After spending his early career on Wall Street and as an entrepreneur, Ron Blue became a Christian in his early 30s. Since 1979 he has held a God-given passion to help Christians plan and manage their finances in order to maximize Kingdom giving. Over time Ron has pursued this passion in several different ways. He is the founder of Ronald Blue & Company, now Ronald Blue Trust, the largest fee-only Christian financial-planning form in the country. He has authored 26 books on biblical financial stewardship, including Master Your Money, The Complete Guide to Faith-Based Family Finances, and Surviving the Financial Meltdown. In 2003 he helped establish Kingdom Advisors, a ministry that trains financial advisers to integrate biblical wisdom into their client advice. In 2012 Ron partnered with Indiana Wesleyan University to establish the Ron Blue Institute, dedicated to multiplying the message of biblical financial wisdom in the church and academic sectors through curriculum development and thought leadership.

Ron holds a BS and an MBA from Indiana University., as well as an honorary doctorate in Business Administration from Indiana Wesleyan University. He and his wife, Judy, live in Bloomington, Indiana. They have five children and 13 grandchildren.

MICHAEL BLUE

Michael Blue wrote and developed the Bible study for *God Owns It All.* Michael lives in Austin, Texas, with his wife, Melissa, and their three boys: Nathan, Daniel, and Brooks. He serves as the executive director and general counsel for the Ron Blue Institute for Financial Planning. Prior to his career with the Ron Blue Institute, Michael worked for two years as a financial planner in Southern California, earning his CFP® designation in 2002, and then practiced law for 10 years in Dallas and Austin, Texas. Michael speaks on personal finance and generosity and recently revised and updated Ron's first book, *Master Your Money,* for the 30th anniversary of its first printing. In his spare time Michael is pursuing a master's degree in theological studies. Michael has a passion to see Christians become free in their finances so that they can follow God's leading in their lives and can be free to emulate God's character as givers.

Introduction

God Owns It All is the culmination of my life's experience and work. Beginning as a CPA on Wall Street in the 1960s, I've spent over 50 years thinking about and giving advice on money and finances. After working on Wall Street, then on main street in a private accounting practice, and finally in many parts of Africa as a full-time ministry worker, I founded one of the first fee-only financial-planning firms in the United States, Ronald Blue & Company.

The year was 1979, and my goal in founding the company was to help Christians plan and manage their finances so that they would have more money to give away. Thirty-seven years later Ronald Blue & Company manages over $6.5 billion and serves over seven thousand clients.

What my life's work and passion have taught me is that the Bible authoritatively speaks to our finances today, just as it did yesterday and in the days of King Solomon. The Bible gives us clear direction on how to use our money, and its teachings simply work. With that backdrop in mind, I've created this small-group Bible study to share with you from my years of experience much of what I've learned from the Bible's wise teachings on finances.

Over these next six weeks you'll have the opportunity to wrestle with and answer heart-related questions about the Bible and money. You'll be confronted with foundational questions about money, like: Who owns it? How much is enough? Will it continue to be enough?

I pray that by the end of this Bible study, you'll more completely understand that God's Word is authoritative at all times for all financial planning and decision making, providing supernatural wisdom for the process; timeless, transcendent principles for the decisions; and contentment at all times in all circumstances.

I've seen and experienced the contentment and peace that come from following God's Word and God's principles in my own finances and in the lives of countless clients. I'm confident that if you open your heart to what the Bible has to say about your finances, you'll be able to move from fear and discontentment to contentment and joy. I look forward to taking this journey with you, and I know we'll all be changed by listening and responding to God's Word.

How to Use This Study

This Bible study provides a guided process for individuals and small groups to explore Scriptures that shape a Christian's view of money. This study is divided into six weeks of study:

WEEK 1: PERSPECTIVE
WEEK 2: PRINCIPLES
WEEK 3: LIVE
WEEK 4: GIVE
WEEK 5: OWE
WEEK 6: GROW

One week of Bible study is devoted to each of these topics, and each week is divided into three sections of personal study:

STUDY
REFLECT
APPLY

In these sections you'll find biblical teaching and interactive questions that will help you understand and apply the teaching.

In addition to the personal study, six group sessions are provided that are designed to spark gospel conversations around brief video teachings. Each group session is divided into three sections:

START: This section focuses participants on the topic of the session's video teaching.
WATCH: This section provides key Scriptures and ideas presented in the video and space to take notes.
DISCUSS: This section guides the group in a discussion of the video teaching.

If you want to go deeper in your study, you may want to read the book on which this Bible study is based, *Never Enough?* (B&H Publishing) is ISBN 978-1-4336-9071-6.

Tips for Leading a Small Group

PRAYERFULLY PREPARE

Prepare for each group session with prayer. Ask the Holy Spirit to work through you and the group discussion as you point to Jesus each week through God's Word.

REVIEW the weekly material and group questions ahead of time.

PRAY for each person in the group.

MINIMIZE DISTRACTIONS

Do everything in your ability to help people focus on what's most important: connecting with God, with the Bible, and with one another.

CREATE A COMFORTABLE ENVIRONMENT. If group members are uncomfortable, they'll be distracted and therefore not engaged in the group experience.

TAKE INTO CONSIDERATION seating, temperature, lighting, refreshments, surrounding noise,and general cleanliness.

At best, thoughtfulness and hospitality show guests and group members they're welcome and valued in whatever environment you choose to gather. At worst, people may never notice your effort, but they're also not distracted.

INCLUDE OTHERS

Your goal is to foster a community in which people are welcome just as they are but encouraged to grow spiritually. Always be aware of opportunities to include and invite.

INCLUDE anyone who visits the group.

INVITE new people to join your group.

ENCOURAGE DISCUSSION

A good small-group experience has the following characteristics.

EVERYONE PARTICIPATES. Encourage everyone to ask questions, share responses, or read aloud.

NO ONE DOMINATES—NOT EVEN THE LEADER. Be sure your time speaking as a leader takes up less than half your time together as a group. Politely guide discussion if anyone dominates.

NOBODY IS RUSHED THROUGH QUESTIONS. Don't feel that a moment of silence is a bad thing. People often need time to think about their responses to questions they've just heard or to gain courage to share what God is stirring in their hearts.

INPUT IS AFFIRMED AND FOLLOWED UP. Make sure you point out something true or helpful in a response. Don't just move on. Build community with follow-up questions, asking how other people have experienced similar things or how a truth has shaped their understanding of God and the Scripture you're studying. People are less likely to speak up if they fear that you don't actually want to hear their answers or that you're looking for only a certain answer.

GOD AND HIS WORD ARE CENTRAL. Opinions and experiences can be helpful, but God has given us the truth. Trust Scripture to be the authority and God's Spirit to work in people's lives. You can't change anyone, but God can. Continually point people to the Word and to active steps of faith.

KEEP CONNECTING

Think of ways to connect with group members during the week. Participation during the group session is always improved when members spend time connecting with one another outside the group sessions. The more people are comfortable with and involved in one another's lives, the more they'll look forward to being together. When people move beyond being friendly to truly being friends who form a community, they come to each session eager to engage instead of merely attending.

ENCOURAGE GROUP MEMBERS with thoughts, commitments, or questions from the session by connecting through emails, texts, and social media.

BUILD DEEPER FRIENDSHIPS by planning or spontaneously inviting group members to join you outside your regularly scheduled group time for meals; fun activities; and projects around your home, church, or community.

WEEK 1

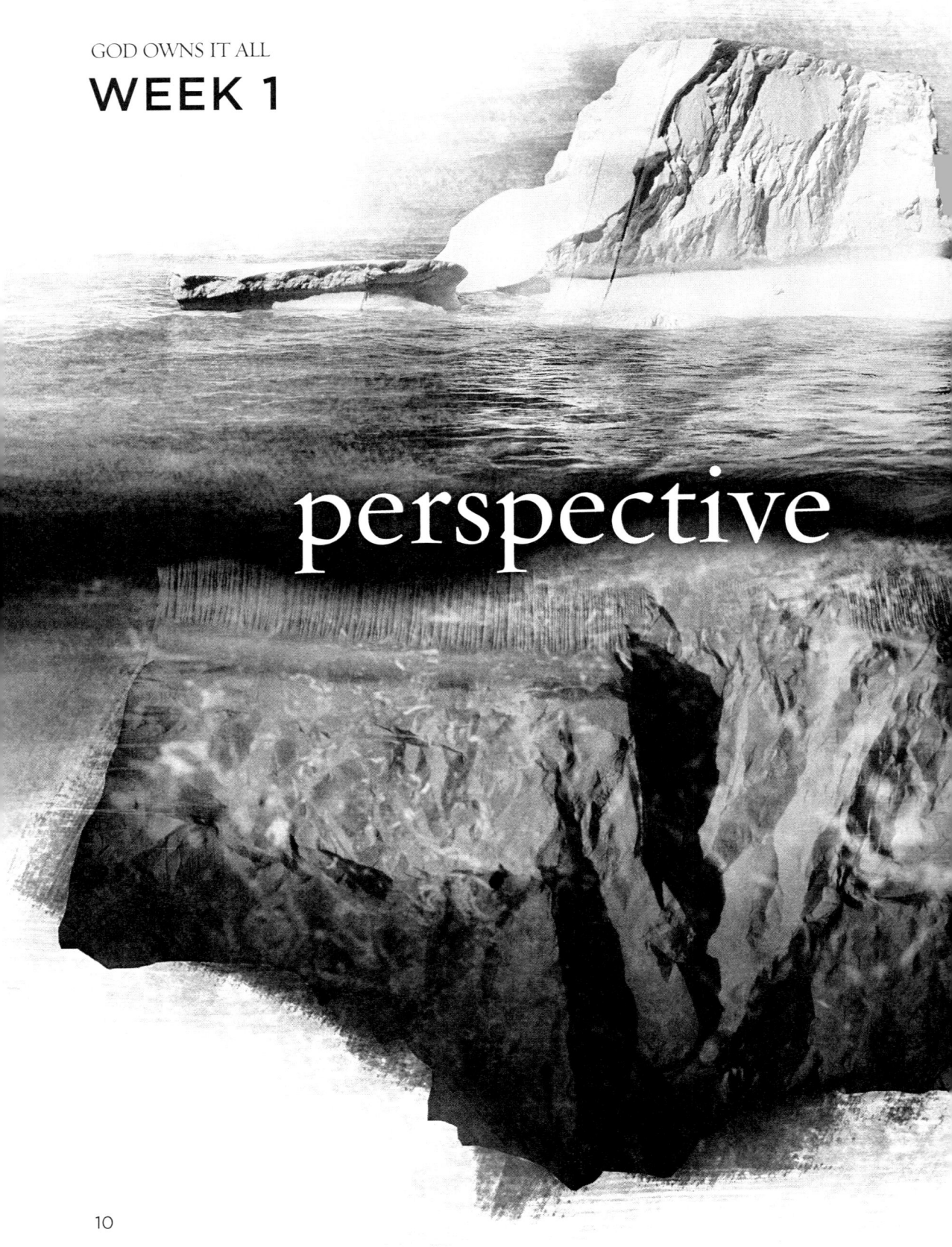

perspective

start

Welcome to session 1 of God Owns It All. *Open the session with prayer. Then briefly discuss the following.*

What childhood experiences or memories have most influenced your view of money or giving?

How are money and contentment connected?

We all tend to believe if we had a little bit more money and could do or buy a few more things, we would experience contentment and peace. We believe more money brings security and security brings contentment. If this is true, then why do so many wealthy people seem so discontent? Does money have anything to do with being content?

Over the next six weeks you'll learn how you can experience contentment in relation to your money, as well as confidence in the way you manage it.

Read Luke 16:10-13 together. Then watch the video for session 1, in which Ron Blue sets the stage for our journey into biblical truths about our roles as managers of God's resources.

watch

Money-Management Principles

1. Spend less than you earn.
2. Avoid the use of debt.
3. Save or build margin for the unexpected.
4. Set long-term goals.
5. Give generously.

God's Word speaks authoritatively to every financial decision—all financial planning, it gives wisdom for the process, it gives principles for the decision, and it works at all times under any circumstances.

Following God's Word in finances will lead to—
- contentment;
- confidence;
- clarity of communication;
- consistency of behavior.

TRANSFERABLE CONCEPT
Behavior always follows a belief system.

All behavior is the product of what we choose to think or believe. ... Trying to change behavior, without changing what we believe and therefore think, will never produce any lasting results.[1]

Neil Anderson

Questions People Want Answered

1. Will I ever have enough?
2. Will it continue to be enough?
3. How much is enough?

Worldview: the overall perspective from which one sees and interprets the world

Driving Forces of Our Worldview

1. Culture
2. God's Word

What the culture says: money will provide a means to success, significance, or security.

Financial Questions from a Biblical Worldview

1. Who owns it?
2. How much is enough?
3. Is the next steward prepared and chosen?

TRANSFERABLE CONCEPT

God owns it, and therefore, I am a steward.

Ways God Uses Money in My Life

1. A tool
2. A test
3. A testimony

> For where envy and selfish ambition exist, there is disorder
> and every kind of evil. But the wisdom from above is first
> pure, then peace-loving, gentle, compliant, full of mercy
> and good fruits, without favoritism and hypocrisy.
> ### James 3:16-17

> Now if any of you lacks wisdom, he should ask God, who
> gives to all generously and without criticizing, and it will be
> given to him. But let him ask in faith without doubting. For the
> doubter is like the surging sea, driven and tossed by the wind.
> ### James 1:5-6

TRANSFERABLE CONCEPT

The eternal perspective will always lead to
contentment, regardless of the circumstances.

---

1. Neil T. Anderson, *The Bondage Breaker* (Eugene, OR: Harvest House, 1990), 69.

discuss

Ron quoted these words by Neil Anderson:

> All behavior is the product of what we choose
> to think or believe. ... Trying to change behavior,
> without changing what we believe and therefore
> think, will never produce any lasting results.[1]
>
> *Neil Anderson*

Was there a time in your life when you tried to change your behavior without fully committing to the reason for the change? What was your experience with that intended change over time?

What do you think most people believe is the primary purpose of money?

Often people think they can find success, security, and significance in having more money. However, when we look at people with a lot of money, we don't necessarily see evidence that this is true.

What makes us believe money can help us become successful, secure, or significant?

Think about one of these three measures: success, security, and significance. Now think about a person you've known who most strongly exhibited this trait. Share with the group what you believe made that person highly successful, significant, or secure.

Ron taught the transferable concept that behavior always follows our belief system. The biggest shaping influence of our belief system is our worldview.

Has your faith changed your worldview? If so, in what ways?

A biblical worldview says God owns my money, and therefore, I'm a steward of it. A cultural worldview says my money is mine, and I can do whatever I want with it.

How have you seen the tension between these views play itself out?

If the money you have is really God's money, what implications does that have for the way you use it?

Having a biblical worldview means having an eternal perspective. An eternal perspective will always lead to contentment, regardless of the circumstances. Read Matthew 6:19-20.

What does a contented person look like?

How can having an eternal perspective lead you to be more content with what you have?

Do you believe you can be content with what you have?

In closing, pray and thank God for entrusting His children with resources to manage and distribute.

1. Neil T. Anderson, *The Bondage Breaker* (Eugene, OR: Harvest House, 1990), 69.

study

I remember when my kids were still living under my roof and first experiencing the freedom that comes with the ability to drive. The look of sheer joy on their faces when they first got their licenses was a sight to see. I could almost sense their newfound feeling of freedom and independence. I knew, however, that in order for them to truly experience the freedom that comes with driving, they needed to have access to a car.

This is where I came in to kill the joy. (That's the primary role of a parent, right?) Judy and I decided it would be good for our family if our kids had access to a car when they reached driving age. So when our oldest turned 16, we bought an extra car. We gave our kids full access to that car to use at their convenience. There was a catch though: if we needed them to give one of the other kids a ride or to run an errand for us, they were expected to do so. I often reminded them that the car was "Dad's car, for Dad's convenience."

I had given them full access to a car, but it was still my car. They could use it without getting my approval, but when I needed them to use it for my convenience or the convenience of the family, they were expected to do so. The key issue was ownership. Once the kids understood the ownership and the responsibilities of using the car, everyone got along great (well, most of the time).

"Who owns it?" is one of the key questions every Christian must answer about money and resources. The answer to this question has the potential to transform every financial decision we make. I often say every financial decision is a spiritual decision. The reason I say that is based on my belief about who owns it. Though I'm sure you can guess what I believe, let's take a look at what the Bible has to say about who owns our money.

**As you read the following verses,
underline everything God owns.**

Who am I, and who are my people, that we should be able
to give as generously as this? For everything comes from You,
and we have given You only what comes from Your own hand.
I Chronicles 29:14

The earth and everything in it,
the world and its inhabitants,
belong to the LORD.

Psalm 24:1

I will not accept a bull from your household
or male goats from your pens,
for every animal of the forest is Mine,
the cattle on a thousand hills.
I know every bird of the mountains,
and the creatures of the field are Mine.
If I were hungry, I would not tell you,
for the world and everything in it is Mine.

Psalm 50:9-12

**What are the implications for your life
of God's ownership of everything?**

Scripture is very clear about who owns the earth and all the rest of creation. The problem most of us have isn't with acknowledging that God owns the earth; it's acknowledging that God owns our stuff. For some reason it's much easier to think the trees and the animals belong to God, but when God's ownership extends to our possessions, we find it much harder to bel eve God owns it all. However, Scripture is very clear that everything on the earth is the Lord's, including all our personal possessions.

Let's briefly look at some of the dangers of not believing this truth.

**In the following passage draw a box around
everything God did for the Israelites. Circle
everything the Israelites did for themselves.**

When you eat and are full, you will praise the LORD your God for the good land He has given you. Be careful that you don't forget the LORD your God by failing to keep His command— the ordinances and statutes—I am giving you today. When you eat and are full, and build beautiful houses to live in, and your herds and flocks grow large, and your silver and gold multiply, and everything else you have increases, be careful that your heart doesn't become proud and you forget the LORD your God who brought you out of the land of Egypt, out of the place of slavery. He led you through the great and terrible wilderness with its poisonous snakes and scorpions, a thirsty land where there was no water. He brought water out of the flint-like rock for you. He fed you in the wilderness with manna that your fathers had not known, in order to humble and test you, so that in the end He might cause you to prosper. You may say to yourself, "My power and my own ability have gained this wealth for me," but remember that the LORD your God gives you the power to gain wealth, in order to confirm His covenant He swore to your fathers, as it is today. If you ever forget the LORD your God and go after other gods to worship and bow down to them, I testify against you today that you will perish. Like the nations the LORD is about to destroy before you, you will perish if you do not obey the LORD your God.

Deuteronomy 8:10-20

How has God provided for you? List the ways.

Why was it important for the Israelites not to forget that God was their provider?

Tremendous temptation and danger threaten us when we fall into the trap of believing we're responsible for our own success. The world tells us we can be anything we want to be. This isn't 100 percent true. Rather, we can be anything God created us to be. We have a responsibility to cultivate the gifts, resources, and abilities we've been given to the very best of our abilities, but we can't forget the source of those gifts, resources, or abilities. I'm 5 feet 9 inches tall with a minimal vertical leap and average quickness (I'm also over 70). I couldn't have been a professional basketball player, even in my prime, no matter how hard I worked. God didn't create me that way. However, I was gifted in other ways. I view these gifts as coming from the Lord, and I believe it's my responsibility to use them to my fullest.

List the abilities and accomplishments of which you're proudest.

Reflect on the origins of these abilities and the sacrifices others made to help you achieve your accomplishments.

If you're willing to be 100 percent honest with yourself, you'll realize that the reasons you're successful are the skills you were born with and the circumstances in which you were raised. We received all these things by God's sovereign grace. Recognizing the truth that God is the owner of all our resources leads us to view ourselves as stewards and not owners. A steward is simply a manager for someone else.

My personal, long-standing definition of *stewardship* is:

The use of God-given gifts and resources—such as time, talent, treasure, influence, and relationships—for the accomplishment of God-given goals and objectives

The biggest mental shift most people have to make when they move from an owner perspective to a steward perspective comes in the area of accountability. If our money and resources are God's, that means He cares what we do with them. If He cares what we do with them, that means we should always consult Him about our decisions.

Let's look at one of the most important passages on stewardship in the Bible, the parable of the talents.

Read Matthew 25:14-30.

This parable contains many great teaching points. Although it's primarily about the kingdom of God, it teaches us some key principles about stewardship.

THE AMOUNT WE HAVE ISN'T IMPORTANT

**In verses 14-18 how did the master
decide to distribute the talents?**

**In verses 19-23 did the master respond differently
to the slave with two talents and the one with
five talents? What did he say to each one?**

While it's easy to say, "It's not fair" about one steward getting five and one getting two, it's also interesting to note that the master responded exactly the same way to both of the stewards, indicating that he wasn't rewarding the amount they used or multiplied; rather, he was interested in the wise use of the resources they had.

FAITH REQUIRES ACTION

**In verses 24-27 what did the slave with one
talent do wrong? Was he treated fairly?**

The evil, lazy slave knew better but did nothing. He didn't have an active, faithful approach to stewarding the resources he was given. He lived by his feelings (fear) rather than by the truth (the master would come back expecting well-cared-for resources).

WE'RE BEING PREPARED FOR SOMETHING BETTER

How do your life and your use of resources demonstrate the value you place on eternity?

Which of these servants do you view as most similar to you? Why?

To sum it up, you can't fake stewardship. The slave with the one talent couldn't pretend he had done something with that talent when it was obvious he had done nothing. Once you've acknowledged that God owns it all and that you're a steward of His resources, your mentality should change about every financial decision. All of a sudden it becomes important what the master (God) says you should do with your resources. It's all His, and He cares what you do with it.

Take a look at your bank statement or credit-card statement and ask yourself, *What do my spending decisions say about what I value most?*

Spend a few minutes thanking God for all He has blessed you with: time, talent, resources, family, relationships, church, and so on. Ask Him how He wants you to use those gifts for His glory.

reflect

In the book *Counterfeit Gods* Timothy Keller talks about the dangers of greed and the difficulty people have recognizing it in their own lives. One point he made that has stuck with me for many years is that as a pastor, he's had people come and confess to him every sin imaginable, but not once has he ever had someone sit down in his office and say, "I spend too much money on myself. I think my greedy lust for money is harming my family, my soul, and people around me."[1]

It's interesting to me that it's so hard to identify greed in my own life. I imagine it's equally hard for you. If I told a lie about something, I would know it right away, but with greed it's more insidious and difficult to identify. When we fail to notice it, we fail to understand how greed drives our behavior and decision making.

In the video for this session, I showed a picture of an iceberg and talked about the importance of understanding our worldview and why we do the things we do. I said the *why* matters more than the *how*. We'll talk about the *how* in the later sessions, but honestly, the *how* makes very little difference if we don't understand the *why* behind it. The answer to the *why* question is determined by our worldview.

In this week's "Study" section we looked deeply at what the Bible says about who owns our stuff and the implications of the answer to that question. Assuming we can agree that the Bible clearly teaches that God is the owner of the earth and everything in it, I'd like to take a little more time to look at the different worldviews presented by the Bible and culture.

One of the transferable concepts from the group session this week was that an eternal perspective will always lead to contentment, regardless of the circumstances. In what ways is this a significant truth in your life, apart from your finances?

How do you see this transferable concept as a significant truth in your life that specifically relates to your finances?

Record on the chart the sources of success, security, and significance, according to our culture and the Bible.

CULTURE	BIBLE
Success	
Security	
Significance	

Where have you looked for success, security, and significance in your life?

We ended the "Study" section with the challenge to look at your bank statement or credit-card statement and ask what your spending decisions say about what you value most. Imagine that you asked a stranger to look at your statements and record the things they think are most important to you. What do you think the stranger would identify?

Are you comfortable with what this stranger would identify? Why or why not?

Culture aggressively tells us that we should be discontented with what we have. Companies spend billions of dollars every year trying to convince us that our lives would be better if we owned their products. In other words, our lives aren't good enough as they are right now. These messages create feelings of discontentment, fear, and uncertainty.

In contrast to a cultural worldview, the Bible offers hope, encouragement, and contentment, even in the face of uncertainty. The Bible provides us with the perspective that we need to be able to approach uncertainty and fear with confidence and clarity. The Bible presents us with an eternal perspective and allows us to rightly focus on that reality, which results in contentment and confidence. Compared to the things of eternity, the things of this world have very little value. When we value eternity, we realize that enough is found in God and not in our wealth. He's enough, and therefore we'll always have enough.

The Bible tells us money can be used for three things.

A TOOL

> I don't say this out of need, for I have learned to be content
> in whatever circumstances I am. I know both how to have a
> little, and I know how to have a lot. In any and all circumstances
> I have learned the secret of being content—whether well
> fed or hungry, whether in abundance or in need. I am able
> to do all things through Him who strengthens me.
>
> ### Philippians 4:11-13

Money can be used as a tool in our lives in a few different ways.

1. Money can be used to accomplish God's objectives.
2. Money can be used to teach us to rely on God.
3. Money can be used to buy things for ourselves or others.

When we use money, we're investing it, not spending it.

How has God used money as a tool in your life?

A TEST

> Whoever is faithful in very little is also faithful
> in much, and whoever is unrighteous
> in very little is also unrighteous in much.
>
> ### Luke 16:10

**Do you think it would be harder to put your trust in God
if you had an abundance of money or if you had a shortage
of money? Which would you view as a greater test?**

We can be tested by having a lot or by having a little. Just because we have a lot of money, we can't automatically assume God has given it to us for our simple enjoyment and pleasure. He may have given it to us to test where we're placing our true worship.

**What would be your reaction if God told you
to sell all you have and give it to the poor?**

A TESTIMONY

You are the salt of the earth. But if the salt should lose its taste,
how can it be made salty? It's no longer good for anything but
to be thrown out and trampled on by men. You are the light
of the world. A city situated on a hill cannot be hidden. No
one lights a lamp and puts it under a basket, but rather on a
lampstand, and it gives light for all who are in the house. In the
same way, let your light shine before men, so that they may
see your good works and give glory to your Father in heaven.
Matthew 5:13-16

How could you use your money to provide a testimony to other people of God's love for you?

Whether you have much or little, the way you handle your money can be a testimony to those around you. Your willingness to trust God when you have little and your willingness to share generously when you have much will both witness to an unbelieving world that Jesus is worthy of all devotion and worship.

If you feel that you've allowed money to control you, that you're failing the test of money, or that your use of money has given a bad testimony, don't beat yourself up. The gospel is a message of good news, and so is the Bible's message about money. Instead of beating yourself up, set a new vision.

Get an index card and record ways you can use your money as a tool and a testimony over the next month. Place that card in a place where you'll see it every time you start to spend money, like your wallet or purse. Let the card remind you of your new vision for spending.

Take a few minutes to ask God to help you see His eternal perspective on money and possessions more clearly.

1. Timothy Keller, *Counterfeit Gods* (New York: Dutton, 2009).

apply

Do you remember the story of the 12 spies Moses sent into the promised land to observe, gather information, and report about the land? Ten of the spies returned to Moses and described being terrified by the giants who lived in the land, while two of the spies, Joshua and Caleb, returned to tell Moses, "We must go up and take possession of the land because we can certainly conquer it!" (Num. 13:30).

The difference between the 10 spies and Joshua and Caleb was a simple thing: their perspective. The 10 believed in the strength of the opponent; the 2 believed in the strength of God. Perspective is everything!

We've spent a lot of time developing a foundational perspective from which you can begin to build your beliefs about money.

The most foundational belief you must establish about money is who owns it. List your things, talents, time, relationships, and anything else God has given you that you may be tempted to consider as your own resources.

If you believe God owns all these things, fill out and sign the following form.

I acknowledge God's ownership of my time, talents, treasure, relationships, influence, and all other resources I listed above. I agree to act as a steward of those things, and I commit to seek God's direction for what to do with His resources.

Signature _____ Date _____

Not only did Joshua and Caleb understand that God was in control and they were His to be used, but they also maintained an eternal perspective. Knowing their ultimate destination was eternity, they were able to keep things here and now in proper perspective. An eternal perspective leads to contentment because it orients everything around our true home and where our true value lies.

As you move through this Bible study, I encourage you to continually return to the question of *why* you're using money the way you do. If you don't have a good understanding of your *why,* then no matter what you learn in this Bible study, you'll eventually fall back into old behaviors and habits.

Take a minute to think about why you want to get a better handle on your money. Then record your *why* beside the iceberg.

Each week provides an opportunity to reflect on what you're learning and the convictions you're developing through your study of biblical teachings on money and stewardship. As Randy Alcorn aptly stated in his book *Money, Possessions and Eternity,* "Nothing is more fleeting than the moment of conviction."[1] I sincerely pray that your conviction today about your financial beliefs can and will lead to transformational change. For that to happen, you must embrace that conviction and pursue change in your habits. The beginning point is to record your convictions and beliefs about money.

Here are my personal convictions on this week's topics:

1. Because God owns everything, I'm simply a steward of what's already His.
2. Stewardship is the only area of the Christian life that can't be faked.
3. The way we spend our money is a measure and reflection of our real priorities.
4. Every spending decision is a spiritual decision.
5. God can take whatever He wants whenever He wants. Believing this is the key to financial freedom.
6. Changed behavior always begins with changed thinking.

In a moment I want you to record your own personal convictions, but first let me offer some guidelines.

Guidelines for personal convictions:

1. I define *conviction* as a well-thought-out resolution between you and God. It's something you're staking your behavior on and something you *know* that you know. Remember the words of Romans 14:5: "Each one must be fully convinced in his own mind."
2. These are your personal convictions, not mine. Your convictions won't be exactly the same as mine.
3. Your convictions will develop and change over time, but at all times they'll lead you into certain behaviors.
4. These are convictions, not rules or regulations. Trust that God will lead you to develop and modify them over time.

**Now record one or two personal convictions
about the topics we discussed this week.**

How do you feel encouraged by what you learned this week?

How do you sense God moving you to change,
based on what you learned this week?

Record ways your belief about who owns your money dictated
your behavior with respect to your money in the past.

How do you see this perspective changing?

Close your time in silence and prayer, listening to what
God is teaching you and asking Him for wisdom in
forming your beliefs about finances and stewardship.

The wisdom from above is first pure, then
peace-loving, gentle, compliant, full of mercy
and good fruits, without favoritism and hypocrisy.
James 3:17

1. Randy C. Alcorn, *Money, Possessions, and Eternity* (Carol Stream, IL: Tyndale, 2003).

principles

start

Welcome to session 2 of God Owns It All. *Open the session with prayer. Then briefly discuss the following.*

What was one point that stood out to you
as you completed last week's personal study?

How does believing you're a steward and not
an owner affect the way you use money?

What tangible steps can you take
to develop an eternal perspective?

Understanding what the Bible says about money is the key to solidifying a biblical worldview and an eternal perspective. The Bible has a lot to say about money. In fact, it contains more than 2,350 verses about finances. Of Jesus' 38 parables, 16 of them are about money.

In this session we'll explore five biblical principles of money management and five uses of money. Knowing and applying these principles will lead us into confidence because we can be sure these principles will never change.

Read 2 Timothy 3:16-17 together. Then watch the video for session 2, in which Ron Blue teaches five biblical money-management principles and discusses the fact that all our financial priorities are simultaneous.

watch

TRANSFERABLE CONCEPT
Applying biblical principles to financial
decisions always leads to confidence.

Biblical principles are always right, they're always relevant, and they're never going to change.

> Therefore, everyone who hears these words of Mine and acts on them will be like a sensible man who built his house on the rock. The rain fell, the rivers rose, and the winds blew and pounded that house. Yet it didn't collapse, because its foundation was on the rock. But everyone who hears these words of Mine and doesn't act on them will be like a foolish man who built his house on the sand. The rain fell, the rivers rose, the winds blew and pounded that house, and it collapsed. And its collapse was great!
>
> Matthew 7:24-27

Steps to Understand Your Finances

1. God owns it all.
2. I'm managing His resources (five money-management principles).
3. There are five uses of money.
4. Sequential investing

Money-Management Principles

1. Spend less than you earn.
2. Avoid the use of debt.
3. Save or build margin for the unexpected.
4. Set long-terms goals.
5. Give generously.

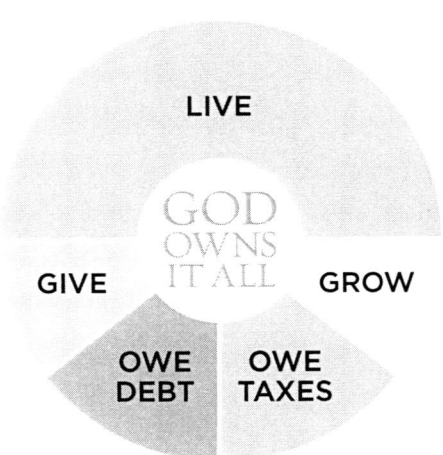

TRANSFERABLE CONCEPT

The priorities in the pie diagram compete
with one another, and they are simultaneous.

There are no independent financial decisions.

If I know the biblical principles of managing money, that leads me to total confidence in the decisions that I'm making, and it gives me the freedom to set my priorities to create consistency of behavior.

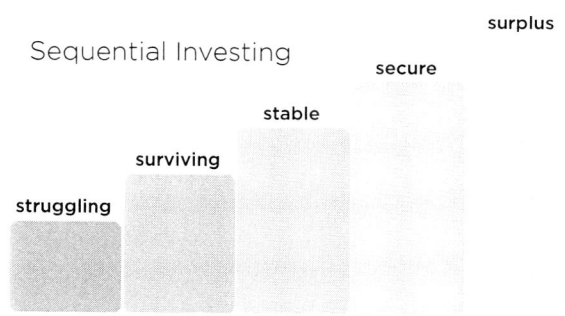

Sequential Investing

surplus

secure

stable

surviving

struggling

All Scripture is inspired by God and is profitable for teaching, for rebuking, for correcting, for training in righteousness, so that the man of God may be complete, equipped for every good work.

2 Timothy 3:16-17

If I take a long-term perspective, I'm probably going to be making a better decision today.

Financial maturity is being able to give up today's desires for future benefits.

discuss

Because we know Jesus doesn't change, we can be confident that the principles in the Bible won't change.

Where has following biblical wisdom shown itself relevant in your life or in the world around you?

What are some hurdles to believing the Bible can speak accurately and authoritatively to today's issues and concerns?

Ron showed a picture of a single house standing after Hurricane Ike decimated Galveston Island, Texas. This picture demonstrated the importance of having a solid foundation and plan for the future. Matthew 7:24-27 says:

> Everyone who hears these words of Mine and acts on them will be like a sensible man who built his house on the rock. The rain fell, the rivers rose, and the winds blew and pounded that house. Yet it didn't collapse, because its foundation was on the rock. But everyone who hears these words of Mine and doesn't act on them will be like a foolish man who built his house on the sand. The rain fell, the rivers rose, the winds blew and pounded that house, and it collapsed. And its collapse was great!
>
> Matthew 7:24-27

What do you consider the rock of your foundation?

How have you seen a good spiritual foundation make a difference in life?

Ron taught us five biblical money-management principles that form the rock on which we can build a solid financial foundation. In describing these five principles, Ron told two stories. One was about the time he shared these principles with Senator Dodd during a congressional-subcommittee hearing. The other was the story of a young couple who lost nearly one-half of their retirement funds in a market downturn. In both stories the five principles served as the central theme.

How do you think you would respond if you lost
half of your retirement in a market downturn?
Do you think you could look back and reflect with
confidence that you had done all you could have done
by following wise money-management principles?

Which one of the five money-management principles is the
hardest to follow? What makes it particularly difficult?

Ron taught that there are only five things we can do with our money: spend it, give it away, pay off debt, pay taxes, and save it. Allocating our money requires us to make choices between simultaneous, competing priorities.

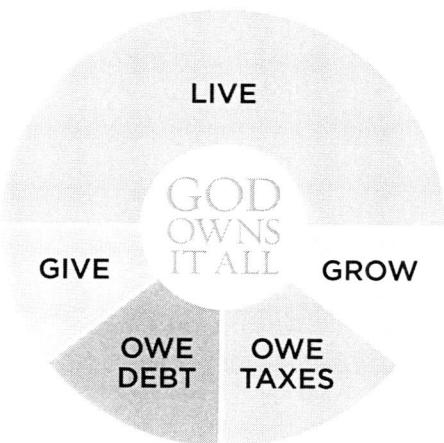

As you look at the pie diagram, which wedge exerts
the most stress or pressure on you? To which wedge
do you wish you could devote more attention?

What are the implications of the statement
"There are no independent financial decisions"?
How does this manifest itself in your life?

In closing, pray and thank God for giving you His Word to guide you in managing the resources He has entrusted to you.

study

In the video for session 2, I told the story of the time I appeared before a congressional subcommittee. Let me take us back there for a moment. I can remember sitting before a bank of microphones, nervous in anticipation of what was about to happen. I was hoping to astonish with my years of wisdom and experience, and then I was asked the question I didn't want to answer. Would I be laughed out of the hearing because of the simplicity of what I was about to say? Hoping I wouldn't be exposed as a simpleton, I swallowed my pride and gave my answer. What followed has given me great confidence in biblical wisdom and truth. A senator asked me to repeat my answer so that he could write it down. I hadn't given him any new wisdom; I had merely told him what the Bible states very simply and clearly. Yet what I had given him was wisdom of the highest form.

There's a huge difference between wisdom and knowledge. Knowledge simply refers to the amount of information stored in our heads, whereas wisdom refers to the framework from which we make decisions. Knowledge represents the *what* and *how,* whereas wisdom represents the *why.* Biblical wisdom is particularly powerful because it's transcendent and timeless. We can be confident in it because it's always right, it's always relevant, and it will never change. This is why I teach principles instead of prescriptions. Principles are based on wisdom, and they're unchanging. They can be applied to anybody in any situation and still be true. They give us confidence in our decisions, and they give us peace, no matter the outcome.

Because we're all bombarded with confusing messages and information overload every day, we need a way to simplify our financial decisions. Today's lesson will equip you with simple tools to address very complex financial issues. It's designed to give you a framework for financial decision making that you can use for the rest of your life. So buckle up and let's see what the Bible has to say about the money-management principles I discussed in the video.

*Spend less than you earn, because every success
in your financial life depends on this habit.*

Read the following Scripture passages and answer the questions.

Idle hands make one poor,
but diligent hands bring riches.
Proverbs 10:4

Wealth gained hastily will dwindle,
but whoever gathers little by little will increase it.
Proverbs 13:11, ESV

God has also given riches and wealth to every man,
and He has allowed him to enjoy them, take his reward,
and rejoice in his labor. This is a gift of God.
Ecclesiastes 5:19

**Read the following statements and place checks beside the true
statements about wealth, based on the Scriptures you read.**
- ☐ **Wealth is a gift.**
- ☐ **Wealth that happens through an
  inheritance or a windfall is best.**
- ☐ **Wealth is the result of diligence.**
- ☐ **Wealth is the result of good fortune.**
- ☐ **Getting rich quickly is dangerous.**
- ☐ **Wealth and work go together.**

**Select one of the true statements that resonates with you. How does
that statement support the idea of spending less than you earn?**

These verses say when we steadily and consistently spend less than we earn over time, the results are increase and abundance. If we don't spend less money than we bring in, it's impossible to achieve any financial goals and to apply any of the other principles. Without margin (the difference between what comes in and what goes out), we can't avoid debt, we can't give, we can't accumulate margin for the unexpected, and our financial goals can't be met. If we don't follow this first principle, we won't have the flexibility or freedom to pursue the goals and objectives that God gives to us.

PRINCIPLE 2

Give generously, because giving breaks the power of money.

Read the following Scripture passages.

A generous person will be enriched,
and the one who gives a drink of water
will receive water.
Proverbs 11:25

I am giving an opinion on this because it is profitable for
you, who a year ago began not only to do something [give
a gift they had pledged] but also to desire it. But now finish
the task as well, that just as there was eagerness to desire it,
so there may also be a completion from what you have.
2 Corinthians 8:10-11

Don't collect for yourselves treasures on earth, where moth
and rust destroy and where thieves break in and steal. But
collect for yourselves treasures in heaven, where neither moth
nor rust destroys, and where thieves don't break in and steal.
For where your treasure is, there your heart will be also.
Matthew 6:19-21

Bring the best of the firstfruits of your land
to the house of the LORD your God.
Exodus 23:19

Giving from the first of our produce and from the ways we've prospered is a biblical concept at the core. We honor God by giving to Him before we know the rest will come in and by giving from our blessing. Giving has tremendous power to free us from the chains of money. We need to be conduits and not containers of the resources God gives us.

PRINCIPLE 3
Avoid debt, because debt always mortgages the future.

Read the following Scripture passages.

The rich rule over the poor,
and the borrower is a slave to the lender.
Proverbs 22:7

The wicked man borrows and does not repay,
but the righteous one is gracious and giving.
Psalm 37:21

Debt is a dangerous master because it will always come calling. We'll explore debt in more detail in a later week, but as a general rule, we should always be very cautious about taking on any debt.

PRINCIPLE 4
Plan for financial margin, because the unexpected will occur.

Read the following Scripture passages.

Go to the ant, you slacker!
Observe its ways and become wise.
Without leader, administrator, or ruler,
it prepares its provisions in summer;
it gathers its food during harvest.
Proverbs 6:6-8

Which of you, wanting to build a tower, doesn't first sit down
and calculate the cost to see if he has enough to complete it?

Luke 14:28

When we fail to set aside something for a short-term emergency, we put our financial lives at risk of collapse. Without margin an unexpected event could spell financial disaster. Be like the ant and set something aside for the winter.

PRINCIPLE 5

Set long-term goals, because there's always a trade-off between the short-term and the long-term.

**Read the following Scripture passages.
Then answer the questions.**

We are His creation, created in Christ Jesus for good works, which
God prepared ahead of time so that we should walk in them.

Ephesians 2:10

I pursue as my goal the prize promised
by God's heavenly call in Christ Jesus.

Philippians 3:14

**If God prepares for things ahead of time
for us to walk in, why should we set goals?**

**How does setting long-term goals change your
short-term perspective on the way you use money?**

When we follow wise financial principles like these, we're able to accomplish our goals or priorities. If we haven't stated these goals or verbalized these priorities, we won't be able to apply financial wisdom to our life's purposes and allow money to be a tool that helps take us where God wants us to go.

Why do you think God encourages us to live by biblical principles? What does this say about His desires for us?

With these principles we're beginning to build a foundational rock for our financial future. This rock of principles says we can build our house by spending less than we earn, giving generously, avoiding the use of debt, creating short-term savings, and setting long-term goals. Psalm 127:1 says:

Unless the LORD builds a house,
its builders labor over it in vain.

Psalm 127:1

Spend a few minutes thanking God for providing you with wisdom and guidance for your life and finances. Ask Him how He wants you to apply these principles to your life.

reflect

A friend of mine at church offers a great example of the transformative effects of applying the five money-management principles we're exploring this week. From the outside this friend, in his early 50s, appears very successful. He has a nice home, a recreational vehicle, two nice cars, a motorcycle, and many of the accoutrements that go with these things. However, his net worth is negative. He owes more than he owns. He has nearly four hundred thousand dollars in debt, while his assets are worth about three hundred thousand dollars. By reading one of my books and listening to a sermon series at our church, he was confronted with the truth of God's Word and these principles. He realized his reason for acquiring many of his toys was to give others the impression that he was wealthy. His money issues were, in fact, heart issues manifesting themselves as pride.

Once my friend recognized his heart issues, he and his wife sat down and prayerfully considered where they were financially, where they wanted to be, and where God wanted them to be. They determined that they wanted to begin tithing and to get out of debt. With these goals in mind, they had two basic choices: (1) begin a payment plan to pay off all their debt over the next 10 years or (2) sell their debt-laden toys and use that money to repay the debt. Both of these choices would put them in great shape, but in either case the couple had to be willing to make sacrifices.

One of the key concepts that helped my friend see where he was spending his money and where he needed to make changes was the pie diagram I introduced in the video. The pie diagram illustrates that there are only a few things we can do with our money: live on it, give it away, owe debt, owe taxes, or use it to grow. You can easily remember those choices by using this rhyming phrase:

LIVE, GIVE, OWE, GROW

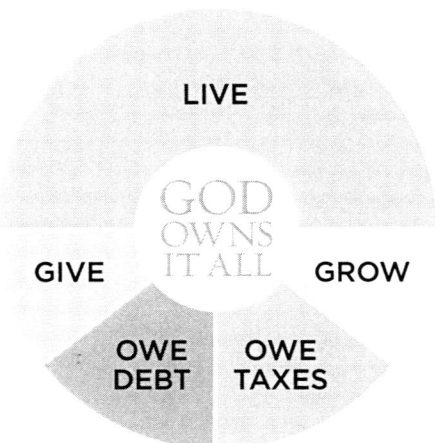

The pie diagram can teach us quite a few truths. It's the simplest budgeting tool I've ever seen. Anybody anywhere can get a general idea of exactly hcw their money is spent if they have five pieces of information from any time period, such as a given month or year:

1. How much money they made
2. How much money they gave away
3. How much money they paid toward debt
4. How much money they paid in taxes
5. How much money they saved

Fill out the following chart for a time period you choose. Don't worry about being perfect or exact. Feel free to make estimates or guesses, but try to be as accurate as you can. For debt, don't include your home mortgage, but include all other types of debt. You'll use these figures to complete your own pie diagram.

LIVE, GIVE, OWE, GROW

Time period (for example, last year, this year to date, last month):

1. What was your income?

2. How much did you give?   *Give:*

3. How much did you pay toward debt?   *Owe debt:*

4. How much did you pay in taxes?   *Owe taxes:*

5. How much did you save?   *Grow:*

Subtract lines 2–5 from your income (line 1) to calculate Live.   *Live:*

To calculate what percentage of your income is used for each piece of the pie, divide each category by your income (for example, $10 of Give / $100 of income = 10 percent). Now calculate your numbers and fill in your pie diagram.

Give percentage: _____

Owe-debt percentage: _____

Owe-taxes percentage: _____

Grow percentage: _____

Live percentage: _____

How do you like the way your pie diagram looks?

What surprises you most about your pie diagram (good or bad)?

I'm really excited about this pie diagram and all the information it reveals. The biggest thing I learn when I look at my pie diagram is that all my priorities are competing and simultaneous. In other words, if I want to save more (that is, make that piece of the pie bigger), one or more of my other pieces of the pie have to get smaller. I can't meet all my goals at the same time unless I have sufficient cash flow to do so, which is admittedly rare.

The other fact a pie diagram illustrates well is that I have limited resources. Your pie may be bigger or smaller than my pie, but regardless of the sizes of our pies, they're finite. Even Bill Gates's pie has a limit to it. Because my resources are limited, I must allocate my resources against competing alternatives. Knowing these two things helps me navigate financial decisions on a daily basis.

The pie diagram reveals three truths:

1. There's no such thing as an independent financial decision.
2. The longer term your perspective, the better your decision today.
3. Financial maturity is being able to give up today's desires for future benefits.

Tying together the five money-management principles, the five uses of money shown on the pie diagram, and the five stages of finances (shown on the diagram below) allows us to create a holistic picture.

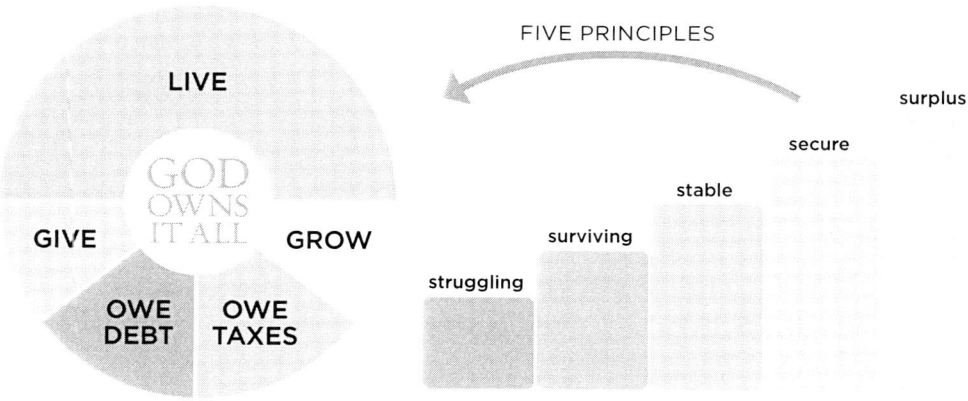

When you apply the five principles to your pie diagram, you can make progress through the five stages, which we'll discuss in week 6. Once you know where you are, you can determine where you want to be and where God wants you to be. Knowing how all these tools work together shows us where we're headed in this study. These simple tools enable us to make sense of our finances so that we can develop a plan to prioritize and give attention to the things God calls us to do.

To make these principles come to life and work effectively, we must understand the concept that all our priorities surrounding our use of money are simultaneous, competing priorities. There's no right sequence for everyone, and sometimes our priorities seem irreconcilable.

Read the account of Elijah and the widow in 1 Kings 17:8-16.

This is a remarkable story. Elijah, in obedience to God, went to a town where he met a widow. This widow had only enough food to make one final meal for herself and her son. Elijah asked her to do something that seems so selfish and unreasonable that it baffles us. Nonetheless, when Elijah was done with his request, he had presented this woman with two competing priorities for all her earthly possessions. The widow had to choose either to obey the prophet of God and feed him first or to feed herself and her son one more meal. If she fed Elijah, there was a chance she would have nothing left to feed herself or her son. If she fed herself and her son, she risked disobeying God and missing out on the miracle Elijah had promised. What would you do?

This choice illustrates the types of competing choices we have to make every day with our money. Feeding her family and feeding Elijah were both worthwhile uses of the widow's food. However, she didn't have enough to do both. Therefore, she had to make a choice.

Understanding the dilemma of competing choices is essential to applying the five money-management principles. The greatest risk inherent in these dilemmas is that we'll permit the struggle to choke out our progress and goals. I'm reminded of the parable of the sower (see Mark 4:1-9,13-20). In Jesus' parable seeds were sown in four different types of soil. Some of the seeds fell among the thorns and were choked out. Jesus said the seeds that fell among the thorns:

> … are the ones who hear the word, but the worries of this age, the seduction of wealth, and the desires for other things enter in and choke the word, and it becomes unfruitful.
> Mark 4:18-19

We all run the risk of allowing competing priorities for the use of our money to choke out the miracles God wants to perform in our lives. When we're faced with simultaneous, competing priorities, our first question should always be "God, what do You want me to do?"

That's the approach taken by the widow asked in the story of Elijah, and as a result, she got to experience a miracle. I imagine that question is what the person who was represented by the fourth soil in the parable of the sower asked every day. This person heard God's direction; welcomed it; and produced a 30-fold, 60-fold, and 100-fold return (which is equivalent to a 3,000 percent, 6,000 percent, and 10,000 percent return). Talk about an effective use of money!

How have you seen simultaneous, competing priorities choke out your growth in Christ?

What are some simultaneous, competing financial priorities you're facing today that need to be brought before God?

Let's briefly return to the story of the couple in my church and reveal what they decided to do. Initially, this couple determined they would adjust their lifestyle and pay off their debts over the next 10 years. However, after an extended time of prayer, the husband felt God leading him to sell their toys and immediately pay off as much debt as they could. This was a very difficult decision, requiring the couple to rely on God for its implementation.

Not long after the couple had made this decision, the wife came up to my wife in tears and told her she had been praying for this moment for 30 years. Her husband had been trapped by the allure of these things and was finally experiencing freedom for the first time. This outcome was possible only because they had recognized where they were and why they were there. Their issue wasn't really a money issue; it was a heart issue. Once their heart problems were properly diagnosed, they were able to use the pie diagram and the principles to develop a plan.

Spend time in prayer. Ask God to give you a willingness to maintain a long-term perspective in your financial life and to move toward the ways He wants you to allocate and use your resources.

apply

Have you ever heard of the butterfly effect? This concept simply states that small causes can have large effects. The analogy goes something like this. If a butterfly flaps its wings in Asia, that small disturbance of wind will ultimately determine when and how a hurricane forms in the Atlantic Ocean weeks later.

The phrase has been used in and outside scientific contexts, but it had its origin in chaos theory. This fact creates an appropriate analogy to finances in a few ways. Not only is *chaos* the word many of us would use to describe our financial situations, but the idea that small causes can have large effects is also a fundamental concept in understanding the money-management principles outlined this week.

The five money-management principles and the pie diagram we've studied highlight the idea that small changes in our financial and spiritual lives can have dramatic results. We'll talk about the magic of compounding in weeks 5–6, but it's important for us to understand that when we make small changes in our finances, we can end up in a dramatically different place 10 or 20 years down the line. Just think about choosing to make your coffee at home instead of buying it at a coffee shop every day. The cost difference may be only $1.50 a day, but that $1.50 a day is actually $547.50 a year and $10,950 over 20 years. Imagine the other uses this money could be put to.

Beside the pie diagram, record a few small changes you'd like to make in your wedges and dream about bigger changes that could result from those small changes.

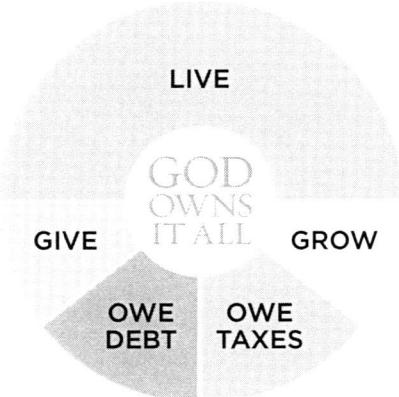

Why is it important for you to make these changes?

Where will the changes you listed have the biggest impact in your life (for example, your heart, spending, or perspective)?

How will these changes help you move to the step on the financial-stages diagram where you feel God is leading you? Indicate on the diagram the step where you are now and the step where you want to be.

Sequential Investing

surplus

secure

stable

surviving

struggling

These types of small changes take a tremendous amount of discipline and persistence. In the video session we talked about financial maturity— being willing and able to give up today's desires for future benefits. The decision whether to buy a cup of coffee every day is a perfect example of this maturity. The challenge with implementing a change like this is that it's so easy to forget why we're doing it.

As you learned in week 1, it's important to spend time solidifying and memorializing your convictions from each week's study. Here are my personal convictions on the topics we've discussed this week:

Here are my personal convictions on this week's topics:

1. There are five planning principles for financial success:
   • Spend less than you earn.
   • Give generously.
   • Avoid the use of debt.
   • Plan for financial margin.
   • Set long-term goals.

2. There are three financial decision-making principles:
   • There's no such thing as an independent financial decision.
   • The longer term your perspective, the better your decision today.
   • Financial maturity is being able to give up today's desires for future benefits.

3. God has given me a pie of a certain size that I'm responsible to allocate and use.

4. God has given me the exact size of pie He wants for me. I need to be thankful for what He has given me.

5. Knowing biblical principles for financial decision making gives me confidence to make decisions and live with the results.

Write one or two personal convictions
from the topics we discussed this week.

How do you feel encouraged by what you learned this week?

How do you sense God moving you to change,
based on what you learned this week?

Identify the principles we discussed this week that, if followed,
would have the biggest impact on your financial future.

Close your time in silence and prayer, listening to what God
is teaching you and asking Him for wisdom in using money.

The wisdom from above is first pure, then
peace-loving, gentle, compliant, full of mercy
and good fruits, without favoritism and hypocrisy.
James 3:17

live

start

Welcome to session 3 of God Owns It All. *Open the session with prayer. Then briefly discuss the following.*

What was one point that stood out to you as you completed last week's personal study?

Which of the money-management principles, if followed, would have the biggest impact on your life today?

In this session we'll explore the Live piece of the pie diagram. In one sentence how would you describe an appropriate Christian lifestyle?

We're all unique. Just as we were all created uniquely, each of our pie diagrams probably looks very different. The biggest variable in most people's pie diagram is the lifestyle wedge, or Live.

Whether we have a really big pie or a really small pie, making intentional choices in our Live wedge can bring about heart change and a feeling of contentment.

If being intentional with respect to our lifestyle is an important step toward feeling content, should everyone live an identical lifestyle?

Read 1 Timothy 6:6-10 together. Then watch the video for session 3, in which Ron Blue addresses the biggest wedge of the pie diagram, Live.

watch

What People Look For

1. Success
2. Significance
3. Security

Lifestyle is the biggest choice we'll make in terms of our finances.

You have to receive in order to give.

How Much Is Enough?

1. The lifestyle that I choose
2. What I have to accumulate in order to maintain that lifestyle

The American Dream does not give you financial freedom. It gives you many, many choices that you have to make.

The Paradox of Prosperity

The more you have doesn't give you more freedom. It may give you less real freedom because now you're confronted with a multitude of choices that you've got to make.

> Your life should be free from the love of money.
> Be satisfied with what you have, for He Himself
> has said, I will never leave you or forsake you.
> ### Hebrews 13:5

What do I need? I need whatever God provides.

If I have an eternal perspective, then I can be content because I know that the future is taken care of.

> I don't say this out of need, for I have learned to be content in whatever
> circumstances I am. I know both how to have a little, and I know how
> to have a lot. In any and all circumstances I have learned the secret of
> being content—whether well fed or hungry, whether in abundance or
> in need. I am able to do all things through Him who strengthens me.
> ### Philippians 4:11-13

If anyone does not provide for his own, that
is his own household, he has denied the faith
and is worse than an unbeliever.
1 Timothy 5:8

What Is the Right Lifestyle for a Christian?

1. Provision
2. Contentment: God wants me to have the necessities of life.
3. Enjoyment

But if we have food and clothing, we will be content with these.
1 Timothy 6:8

Instruct those who are rich in the present age
not to be arrogant or to set their hope on
the uncertainty of wealth, but on God, who
richly provides us with all things to enjoy.
1 Timothy 6:17

The only appropriate Christian lifestyle is the one that God has provided
for me, and I can only determine that by spending time on my knees.

TRANSFERABLE CONCEPT

The only way to increase the pieces of the pie,
excluding your lifestyle, is delayed gratification.

A strange species we are. We can stand
anything God and nature can throw at us save
only plenty. If I wanted to destroy a nation,
I would give it too much and would have it
on its knees, miserable, greedy and sick.[1]

John Steinbeck

1. John Steinbeck, letter to Adlai Stevenson, Guy Fawkes Day 1959, as quoted in *Letters of Note*
[online, cited 28 April 2016]. Available from the Internet: *lettersofnote.com*.

discuss

In the video Ron taught that in order for us to be content with what we have, it's necessary to wrestle with the question "How much is enough?" He proposed two different answers to this question. One is having whatever you want whenever you want it. The other is from Hebrews 13:5, which tells us that enough is exactly what we have right now.

**Have you ever tried to define *enough*
in your life? How did you define it?**

**Why do you think it's so difficult for most of us
to be satisfied with what we have right now?**

It's easy to believe if we had only a little bit more, we would be content. However, if we look at people who have a little or even a lot more than we have, we realize that having more doesn't automatically produce contentment. Read the following verses from Paul's letter to the Philippians.

I have learned in whatever situation I am to be content.
I know how to be brought low, and I know how to abound.
In any and every circumstance, I have learned the secret
of facing plenty and hunger, abundance and need.
I can do all things through him who strengthens me.
Philippians 4:11-13

**What do you think is the process for learning contentment?
What habits or perspectives cultivate contentment?**

What does God's strength have to do with being content?

Lifestyle spending is the biggest consumer of our resources. Ron told a number of stories about people who made the choice to limit their lifestyles as a way to trust God and experience contentment with what they have.

**How would setting a cap on lifestyle spending
lead you into a place of contentment?**

**Do you think there's a single definition of an appropriate
Christian lifestyle that applies to all believers? Why or why not?**

Ron shared three insights from 1 Timothy about an appropriate Christian lifestyle. They are provision, contentment, and enjoyment.

**Discuss how you can apply these standards to your life
and how you might face a struggle in applying them.**

Ron talked about the paradox of prosperity: the more you have, the more choices you have; therefore, the more confusing life becomes.

Do you agree with Ron's paradox of prosperity?

**Why do most of us live as if we believe
we can be the exception to this rule?**

Any discussion of lifestyle and contentment can become legalistic when we begin to look for hard and fast rules for exactly how we should live. The important point is to recognize that no lifestyle will ever bring contentment. That comes only from an eternal perspective and a reliance on God.

In closing, pray and thank God for richly providing exactly what you need.

study

Before we dig into this week's Scripture study, take a minute to assess your degree of contentment with what you have.

**Circle a number from 1 to 10 on the scale
to indicate your level of contentment.**

1   2   3   4   5   6   7   8   9   10

Discontent   **Content**

**When was the last time you remember being content?
Describe your surroundings and your circumstances.**

In the late 1970s I was working for Cru (formerly Campus Crusade for Christ), traveling to Africa and training people in leadership. One Saturday morning I was speaking to a pastor in a village on the outskirts of town as we watched a little girl play with a D battery on top of a pile of discarded rocks. What amazed me about this picture was how perfectly happy and contented this little girl appeared. She didn't even seem to know that she was playing with trash on a pile of trash. I couldn't help but wonder what my five kids were doing back in America—likely watching Saturday-morning cartoons and arguing about who got to play with which toys.

In the midst of this beautiful and convicting scene, I asked the pastor a question I had been wrestling with for some time: what he perceived to be the greatest hindrance to the spread of the gospel in that part of Africa. His answer took me off guard. He simply said, "Materialism."

I was floored and honestly didn't fully comprehend his answer, so I asked him to explain. After all, we were watching a kid play with trash on trash. How could materialism be an issue here? The pastor wisely explained to me that in that part of the world, if someone had a one-room hut, they wanted a hut with two rooms. If someone had a mud hut, they wanted a brick one. If they had two cows, they wanted three. And so on.

You see, materialism, the pastor explained to me, isn't about having a lot and wanting more. Instead, it's defined by worshiping what you have and what you want. It's a belief that having more things can bring contentment and joy. It's a sickness that's present in all corners of the world, and it's just as prevalent among the poor as among the rich. We all struggle with materialism in one form or another, and it's a direct violation of a right belief in who God is and what He has done for us.

In the previous paragraph underline the definition of
***materialism.* How does this definition express itself in your life?**

King Solomon is one of the most qualified individuals in the history of the world to speak to the issue of materialism. He's believed to have been one of the wealthiest people ever. He could have whatever he wanted, whenever he wanted it, and he didn't deny himself much of anything. Yet at the end of his ife, he reflected on his accumulation of wealth and his pursuit of pleasure and found it wanting. His thoughts are recorded in the Book of Ecclesiastes:

> [10]The one who loves money is never satisfied with money, and whoever loves wealth is never satisfied with income. This too is futile. [11]When good things increase, the ones who consume them multiply; what, then, is the profit to the owner, except to gaze at them with his eyes? [12]The sleep of the worker is sweet, whether he eats little or much, but the abundance of the rich permits him no sleep. [13]There is a sickening tragedy I have seen under the sun: wealth kept by its owner to his harm. [14]That wealth was lost in a bad venture, so when he fathered a son, he was empty-handed. [15]As he came from his mother's womb, so he will go again, naked as he came; he will take nothing for his efforts that he can carry in his hands.
>
> Ecclesiastes 5:10-15

Fill in the blanks in verse 10: "The one who _____
money is never _____ with money."
If this is true, why do you think so many of us behave as
though more money will bring us satisfaction or contentment?

Fill in the blanks in verse 13: "There is a grievous evil that
I have seen under the sun: _____ were _____ by their
owner to his _____." What do you think that means?

I often say you never see a hearse pulling a U-Haul. This is a way of saying we'll all depart this world as naked as the day we were born, devoid of any possessions we've accumulated during our lives.

How does keeping a perspective that you can't
take any of your stuff with you when you die enable
you to combat the tyranny of materialism?

List the five things you own that you value most.

1. _____

2. _____

3. _____

4. _____

5. _____

List the five things you own that are most burdensome to you.

1. _____

2. _____

3. _____

4. _____

5. _____

**Record any common threads in either list.
Are the possessions that are most valuable
also the most expensive?   Yes   No
Why or why not?**

Isn't it ironic that having more makes us want even more? This unhealthy desire for more can be combated with the Word of God and with a generous heart:

Your life should be free from the love of money. Be satisfied with what you have, for He Himself has said, I will never leave you or forsake you.
Hebrews 13:5

**What reason does this verse give us
for being satisfied with what we have?**

You're probably familiar with Philippians 4:13: "I am able to do all things through Him who strengthens me." Read this verse in the context of the two preceding verses:

I have learned to be content in whatever circumstances I am.
I know both how to have a little, and I know how to have a lot.
In any and all circumstances I have learned the secret of being
content—whether well fed or hungry, whether in abundance or in
need. I am able to do all things through Him who strengthens me.
Philippians 4:11-13

**What did Paul identify as requiring
the strength of Christ to accomplish?**

While it's easy to say we need to be content with what we have, Paul tells us he learned to be content. Contentment and freedom from materialism are learned behaviors. This means we're on a journey, and we can move along the scale from discontent to content. We shouldn't expect to get there overnight, but we should start moving in that direction.

People can move from discontentment to contentment in two significant ways.

BELIEVING AND RELYING ON GOD'S PROMISE THAT HE WILL NEVER LEAVE THEM OR FORSAKE THEM. The first way is hard to quantify, but it starts with the simple decision to believe God when He says He will never leave you or forsake you (see Heb. 13:5).

Read Matthew 6:26-30 and summarize
Jesus' message in one sentence.

Do you believe God is faithful to His Word
in your life today?   Yes   No

ANSWERING THE QUESTION "HOW MUCH IS ENOUGH?" "Enough for what?" you may ask. Good question. The "How much is enough?" question can apply to many areas of life, but in this context the question is "How much is enough for your lifestyle?"

In week 2 you completed a pie diagram based on what you're spending now. The Live wedge of the pie diagram is usually the biggest slice of the pie and is usually the biggest barrier to financial security.

How do you feel about the size of your Live wedge?

In what way would you like it to look different?

In week 2 we also talked about five biblical principles of money management. The first principle was "Spend less than you earn, because every success in your financial life depends on this habit." This principle comes to life most when we examine our lifestyle.

Over the years I've observed that most people try to apply this principle by earning more money instead of adjusting their lifestyle. Most people think the solution to their financial problems will come by making more money and having more to spend. The truth is that the application of this principle must come from the first two words: "Spend less." You have two choices with this principle: spend less than you earn or spend more than you earn. Only one choice is biblical and will allow you to reach your goals.

I've found that if a person doesn't spend less than they earn on a certain income, raising that income usually doesn't change anything. The question of how much is enough for your lifestyle has already been answered for you: it's determined by how much you make. First Timothy 6 gives a great picture of how the Bible defines *enough:*

> Godliness with contentment is a great gain.
> For we brought nothing into the world,
> and we can take nothing out.
> But if we have food and clothing,
> we will be content with these.
> But those who want to be rich fall into temptation, a trap,
> and many foolish and harmful desires, which plunge people
> into ruin and destruction. For the love of money is a root of
> all kinds of evil, and by craving it, some have wandered away
> from the faith and pierced themselves with many pains.
> 1 Timothy 6:6-10

Record some ways this passage applies to your life.

Spend a few minutes thanking God for providing you with food and clothing. Ask Him to help you believe that He will always care for you and that He's better than any of your desires.

reflect

Contentment and satisfaction are two of the most difficult things to learn in life. I constantly try not to be swayed by culture, and it's a constant battle. I'm sure you battle cultural messages of discontentment too.

C. S. Lewis said it best:

> We are half-hearted creatures, fooling about with drink and sex and ambition when infinite joy is offered us, like an ignorant child who wants to go on making mud pies in a slum because he cannot imagine what is meant by the offer of a holiday at the sea. We are far too easily pleased.[1]

Eternity is far better than anything on earth. Don't be too easily pleased.

**What does it look like in your financial life
to be "far too easily pleased"?**

**In the video session I briefly talked about an appropriate
lifestyle for a Christian. Think about the three
components from 1 Timothy—provision, contentment,
and enjoyment—and then answer the questions.**

PROVISION

If anyone does not provide for his own, that is his own household,
he has denied the faith and is worse than an unbeliever.
1 Timothy 5:8

Think about the different kinds of things you bought over the past month. On the chart designate each category of your purchase as a need or a want.

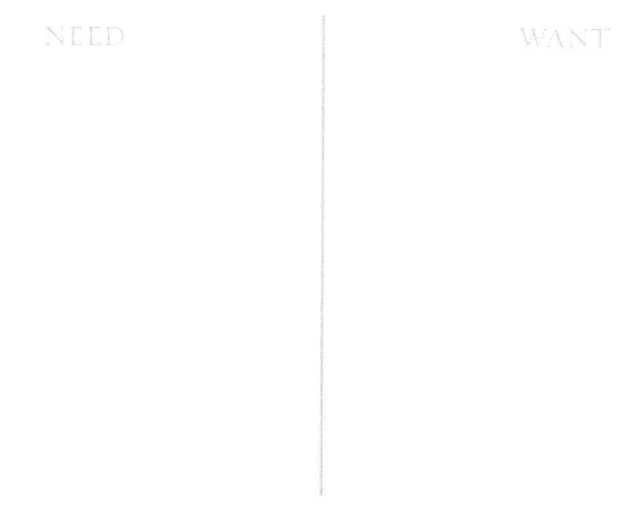

NEED | WANT

How do you define what it means to provide for your family?

Do you think your definition of *provision* should include only needs, or should it also include wants?

CONTENTMENT

If we have food and clothing,
we will be content with these.
1 Timothy 6:8

**What would being content free you
to be and do for God's kingdom?**

ENJOYMENT

Everything created by God is good, and nothing
should be rejected if it is received with thanksgiving.
1 Timothy 4:4

Enjoyment is one of the most frequently forgotten and overlooked areas in Christian finances. It's OK to enjoy what God has given you. In fact, it's wrong not to show gratitude and thanksgiving for what God has blessed you with. Part of that gratitude comes in enjoying what you've been given. James wrote:

Every generous act and every perfect gift is from
above, coming down from the Father of lights; with
Him there is no variation or shadow cast by turning.
James 1:17

Do you enjoy your current lifestyle?   Yes   No
Why or why not?

List three ways you can enjoy the things
God has given you today or this week.

1. _____

2. _____

3. _____

What's the connection among thankfulness,
contentment, and enjoyment?

It's impossible to be content or to enjoy what you have if you don't have a spirit of gratitude. Have you ever given a child a gift and watched them throw a fit because they didn't get something else they wanted? Conversely, when you see genuine thankfulness for a gift, contentment and enjoyment seem to naturally follow. Try to turn your current financial situation into thankfulness. This may be very hard, but if you can look at your situation with gratitude, your ability to move into a new financial reality will increase exponentially.

On the left side of the chart, identify a present reality of your financial situation. On the right side, express thanks for the situation. For example, you might record "I have a mortgage" on the left and "I have a roof over my head" on the right.

REALITY OF FINANCIAL LIFE	STATEMENT OF GRATITUDE

John Wesley truly embodied the threefold Christian lifestyle of provision, contentment, and enjoyment. He provided for his family, he was content with what he had, and he enjoyed the things he was blessed with. Born in 1703, the 15th of 19 children, he was educated at Oxford and led a movement of holiness. He was so intent on getting the Word of God into the hands of every person that he wrote small booklets and sold them for just pennies. The demand for these booklets was remarkable, and John Wesley became a very rich man. Wesley was a prolific preacher and leader as well. It's said that he rode more than 250,000 miles, gave away more than 30,000 pounds (English currency), and preached more than 40,000 sermons.

John Wesley died at the age of 88 surrounded by friends, with only a few coins left in his name. His philosophy of money is summed up well by his statement "I cannot help leaving my books behind me whenever my God calls me hence; but, in every other respect, my own hands will be my executors."[2] John Wesley had much, and he gave much. He lived a full life completely devoted to God. He lived an exemplary life. Will that be said of us?

My goal in this Bible study isn't just to provide you with scriptural principles and financial guidance. I hope you leave filled with Scripture and practical application. With that in mind, I want to give you an opportunity to closely examine your lifestyle wedge of the pie diagram. In order to take full stock of the size of your Live wedge, you must know how you're spending money. And the only way to know that is to create a budget. I know that's a bad word to many people, but a budget is a great tool for helping you move from where you are to where you want to be.

Many useful budgeting tools are available today. Some are more in-depth than others. Here are some recommended resources, based on your particular needs.

IF THIS DESCRIBES YOU	RECOMMENDED TOOL
Don't want to create a budget but want to track how you're spending your money	*mint.com*
Want to create a budget and want online help	*everydollar.com*
Want to create a budget and enjoy tracking the numbers yourself	*faithandfinance.org* (Resources)
Want to create a financial plan and want in-depth information on budgeting	*Master Your Money*
Want to create a financial plan and want professional help	*faithandfinance.org/planning*

Take a few minutes to ask God to give you wisdom for managing your lifestyle budget in a way that honors Him.

---

1. C. S. Lewis, *The Weight of Glory* (New York: HarperOne, 1976), 26.
2. John Wesley, as quoted in Thabiti M. Anyabwile, *Finding Faithful Elders and Deacons* (Wheaton, IL: Crossway, 2012), 89.

apply

When we consider the expenditures that fall into the Live wedge of the pie diagram, we reach the unavoidable conclusion that in our lifestyle spending we necessarily allocate limited resources among unlimited alternatives. In addition, we have to consider whether the lifestyle we're living honors and obeys God. Needless to say, this is a very difficult area of money management for almost everyone.

Two key principles can help us navigate these struggles:

1. There's no such thing as an independent financial decision.
2. Money is a tool to accomplish other goals and objectives.

How would you describe the interdependence of your financial decisions inside the Live wedge of your pie diagram?

What goals or purposes has money helped you accomplish in your life? List four or five that come to mind.

When you hold on to these two principles, lifestyle decisions become less about what you want to have and more about what you want to accomplish. Money is just a tool to accomplish the goals and objectives that God has given you. From this viewpoint money ceases to be an end in itself and becomes the means to a greater goal.

Select some of your God-given goals and
objectives or write your own.

☐ Creating family memories
☐ Attaining an education in the field of _____
☐ Spending time with friends
☐ Spending time on my hobby: _____
☐ Learning about _____
☐ Experiencing _____
☐ Sharing my love of _____ with others
List your own here:

The people who've best handled these lifestyle questions are the ones who answered the "How much is enough?" and "Who owns it?" questions well.

Alan Barnhart is a man who answered these questions at the beginning of his working life. Alan studied the Bible and came away with an understanding of God's ownership and with a healthy fear of wealth and riches. He was torn between a life in ministry and business but ultimately felt called to the business world, with an understanding that no matter where he worked, he was in full-time ministry. Following this decision, he determined to cap his lifestyle at a predetermined amount and give away everything else. Beginning in the first year of his business, he had excess income that he was able to give away for Kingdom work.

Alan's business grew and grew over time and is now worth hundreds of millions of dollars and gives away over one million dollars each month. His perspective is that God has given his company success not to increase his own lifestyle but to enable him to release millions of dollars into the Kingdom. Throughout his career Alan has maintained his perspective that God owns it all and that wealth can be dangerous. He still lives with a modest lifestyle cap and has resisted the temptation to let that cap creep up. Alan could be worth millions of dollars, but instead he chooses to invest in eternity and store up treasures in heaven. He consistently lives a lifestyle that honors God and acknowledges God's ownership of everything he has.[1]

Often the flip side of this attitude of contentment is fear. Prosperity has led American Christians to fear loss even more. This fear of loss often leads to a loss of faith. The more we have, the tighter we grip it. The tighter we grip it, the more disruptions (like Y2K or the Great Recession, for example) scare us to death. Christians are one of the most fearful groups of people I know. Although we have a clear hope of eternity, we're afraid of losing our earthly assets. Instead, we should be fearless and live with an abandon that shows we believe God will never leave us or forsake us (see Heb. 13:5).

Record some of your most pressing financial fears.

Go back and circle all the fears you think are too big for God to help you with. Be honest. Now describe what needs to happen for you to believe that God is bigger than all your fears.

Here are my personal convictions on this week's topics:

1. Financial contentment results from spending less than we make, not from how much we make.
2. The Bible doesn't make clear an appropriate financial lifestyle. Christians must determine this for themselves.
3. There's no such thing as an independent financial decision.
4. Money is a tool to accomplish other goals and objectives.
5. In our Live wedge of the pie diagram, we necessarily have to allocate limited resources among unlimited alternatives.
6. God gives us resources to enjoy. If we're unthankful and unable to enjoy His gifts, it's hard to find joy in sharing with others what God has given us.

Record one or two personal convictions
from the topics we've discussed this week.

In what specific ways do you feel
encouraged by this week's study?

How do you sense God moving you to change,
based on what you learned this week?

Close your study time in silence and prayer, listening
to what God is teaching you and asking Him for wisdom.

The wisdom from above is first pure, then
peace-loving, gentle, compliant, full of mercy
and good fruits, without favoritism and hypocrisy.
James 3:17

1. To hear Alan tell his story, go to *https://generousgiving.org/god-owns-our-business/*.

WEEK 4

give

start

Welcome to session 4 of God Owns It All. *Open the session with prayer. Then briefly discuss the following.*

What was one point that stood out to you as you completed last week's personal study?

How did last week's study change your perspective on a biblical lifestyle?

In this session we'll explore the Give wedge of the pie diagram. Why do you think the Bible tells us to give?

Giving and *stewardship* are two words that have become associated too closely with capital campaigns and new church buildings. The Bible clearly teaches, however, that these concepts are really about our hearts, and they extend beyond our finances.

In this session we'll learn what the Bible has to say about giving, and we'll explore the freedom and contentment that come from being generous. We'll explore the following question: If giving can bring us joy, contentment, and freedom, why is it so difficult for us to trust God and give back to Him what's already His?

Read Matthew 13:44-46 together. Then watch the video for session 4, in which Ron Blue discusses a biblical perspective on giving.

watch

TRANSFERABLE CONCEPT
Money is a reflection of my heart, and giving is a
reflection of my recognition of God's ownership.

On the first day of the week, each of you is to set something
aside and save in keeping with how he prospers.

1 Corinthians 16:2

Motives for Giving

1. Obedience
2. Giving breaks the power of money.
3. Giving is a recognition of God's ownership.
4. Rewards
5. Love

[19]Don't collect for yourselves treasures on earth, where moth and rust destroy and where thieves break in and steal. [20]But collect for yourselves treasures in heaven, where neither moth nor rust destroys, and where thieves don't break in and steal. [21]For where your treasure is, there your heart will be also. [22]The eye is the lamp of the body. If your eye is good, your whole body will be full of light. [23]But if your eye is bad, your whole body will be full of darkness. So if the light within you is darkness—how deep is that darkness! [24]No one can be a slave of two masters, since either he will hate one and love the other, or be devoted to one and despise the other. You cannot be slaves of God and of money.

Matthew 6:19-24

If I'm believing the world system, that is darkness, but if I believe in the goodness and the grace of the gospel of Jesus Christ, that's where the light is.

The earth and everything in it,
the world and its inhabitants,
belong to the LORD.

Psalm 24:1

Well done, good and faithful slave! You were
faithful over a few things; I will put you in charge
of many things. Share your master's joy!

Matthew 25:21,23

You evil, lazy slave! If you knew that I reap where I haven't sown
and gather where I haven't scattered, then you should have
deposited my money with the bankers. And when I returned
I would have received my money back with interest. So take
the talent from him and give it to the one who has 10 talents.

Matthew 25:26-28

[9]For you know the grace of our Lord Jesus Christ: Though He was rich,
for your sake He became poor, so that by His poverty you might become
rich. [10]Now I am giving an opinion on this because it is profitable for
you, who a year ago began not only to do something but also to desire
it. [11]But now finish the task as well, that just as there was eagerness
to desire it, so there may also be a completion from what you have.

2 Corinthians 8:9-11

THE TREASURE PRINCIPLE
You can't take it with you, but you can send it on ahead.[1]

Randy Alcorn

Tithing is the training wheels of giving.

Where to Give

1. The local church
2. The fulfillment of the Great Commission
3. The poor and needy

If anyone has this world's goods and sees his brother in need but
closes his eyes to his need—how can God's love reside in him?

1 John 3:17

How Much to Give

1. Should: proportionate to my income
2. Could: giving out of something I already have
3. Would: "God, if You would provide, I would give it."

1. Randy Alcorn, *The Treasure Principle* (New York: Multnomah, 2001).

discuss

Having taught giving principles for years, Ron knows this subject is one of the most sensitive topics in managing finances. He stated that he wanted this session to focus on the positive nature of giving and to avoid inducing shame and guilt, which have all too often been used to manipulate giving.

**When you think about giving, what
emotional response do you have?**

Shame • Joy • Guilt • Fear • Other

**Why do you think some people react with skepticism and
doubt when a church or ministry leader talks about giving?**

Giving is another way to apply the principle that God owns it all and we're simply His stewards. Giving positions our hearts to respond in gratitude for God's provision and to surrender to His ownership of all we have.

**Do you think it matters what your motive
for giving is as long as you're obedient?**

What are some motives for giving that you've observed?

**Of the biblical motives that Ron gave
for giving, which one compels you most?**

One of the principles Ron explored in the video is that we should give generously because giving breaks the power of money.

How do you think giving can break the power of money?

Jesus taught us the way this principle works:

> Don't collect for yourselves treasures on earth, where moth
> and rust destroy and where thieves break in and steal. But
> collect for yourselves treasures in heaven, where neither moth
> nor rust destroys, and where thieves don't break in and steal.
> For where your treasure is, there your heart will be also.
> Matthew 6:19-21

Many people refer to the idea presented in these verses as the Treasure Principle. The idea is that your heart follows your money.

**How does being generous put the
Treasure Principle into practice?**

**What do you think it means to "collect for
yourselves treasures in heaven" (v. 20)?**

Referring to our treasure, Randy Alcorn said, "You can't take it with you, but you can send it on ahead."[1] When we recognize that our treasures lie in heaven and not on earth, the question moves from "What's the minimum I have to give to be obedient to God?" to "How can I maximize my treasure where it matters for eternity?"

**Ron said tithing is the training wheels of giving.
What's your response to that statement?**

**What's the most impactful story of generous
giving you've seen, heard, or experienced?**

In closing, ask God to make you aware of the needs around you and to give you a generous heart.

1. Randy Alcorn, *The Treasure Principle* (New York: Multnomah, 2001).

study

Howard Hughes was one of the wealthiest men to have lived in the past two hundred years. He was an aviator, an investor, a filmmaker, a business tycoon, an engineer, a hotelier, and an entrepreneur. Yet he was one of the most eccentric, troubled people you could ever come across. Hughes was known as a pleasure-seeking playboy with an aversion to giving. As he grew older, he accumulated more and more wealth, amassing a fortune of over $2.5 billion.

Despite his substantial wealth, Hughes was known as stingy, self-centered, and selfish, allowing his fortune to create an artificial barrier between himself and all those who cared for him. Even as he suffered tremendously with mental and physical health, he pushed away everybody in his life. Hughes became a recluse and was known to lock himself away in one place for months at a time. By the time of his death, he was practically unrecognizable. He died miserable, sad, and alone. His life was one of selfishness and greed. His wealth became a prison, condemning him to a lonely life and death.

In sharp contrast to Hughes, George Müller lived a life marked by radical generosity, although he began life with a purpose similar to Howard Hughes's and was known for stealing, gambling debts, drunkenness, and lewd stories. However, Müller experienced a spiritual transformation and set out to serve God and bring Him glory.

Müller and his wife were deeply affected by the plight of orphans roaming the streets in their town of Bristol, England. They decided to begin an orphanage and determined that they would never ask for money. Whenever they had a need, they brought it to God and watched Him provide. During his life Müller received over 1.5 million pounds in donations. He directed every pound to serving the orphans in his care. He and his wife cared for more than 10,000 orphans, sharing their lives and Christ with each of them.

When Müller died, he had influenced countless souls and is remembered as one of the greatest men of faith in history. He never held on to what was given to him but invested it in other people, and God always provided for him and the orphans. When any orphan became old enough to leave the orphanage, Müller placed a Bible in the orphan's right hand and a coin in the orphan's left hand.

He prayed with the child and told him that if he clung tightly to what was in his right hand, God would always make sure he had something in his left hand.

Both of these men had what many of us long for. Howard Hughes had great wealth and power; George Müller, great faith and impact. However, in these two contrasting stories we see the destructive force of greed and the life-giving force of generosity. Only one of these men lived a life worth emulating, a life filled with joy and wonder. I recently heard a quotation by a Canadian man named Carey Nieuwhof that fittingly sums up these two stories: "There are no inspiring stories of accumulation, only inspiring stories of sacrifice."

Respond to the previous quotation by explaining why you think we desire to accumulate wealth while at the same time hoping our lives will inspire others.

Let's look at what the Bible has to say about motivations for giving.

GIVING BREAKS THE POWER OF MONEY. Giving affirms God's ownership. As long as I hold on to a thing, I believe I own it. Once I let go of it, I've given up power and control. At this point the power of that thing over my life is broken, and I'm free. Jesus said it this way:

> No household slave can be the slave of two masters,
> since either he will hate one and love the other, or
> he will be devoted to one and despise the other.
> You can't be slaves to both God and money.
> ### Luke 16:13

Think about the slave analogy in this verse. How does giving serve God in a way that breaks us free from the bondage of money?

Do money and God compete for your allegiance? What traits might people mistakenly believe these priorities share?

GIVING IS A WAY TO OBEY GOD. This motive is the primary reason we give: because God tells us to. This may sound similar to the frustrating response our parents often gave us when we asked why we had to do something: "Because I said so." However, the Bible gives us concrete reasons God commands us to give:

> Honor the LORD with your possessions
> and with the first produce of your entire harvest.
> ### Proverbs 3:9

> On the first day of the week, each of you is to set something
> aside and save in keeping with how he prospers, so that
> no collections will need to be made when I come.
> ### 1 Corinthians 16:2

> The King will say to those on His right, "Come, you who are
> blessed by My Father, inherit the kingdom prepared for you from
> the foundation of the world. For I was hungry and you gave Me
> something to eat; I was thirsty and you gave Me something to drink;
> I was a stranger and you took Me in; I was naked and you clothed Me;
> I was sick and you took care of Me; I was in prison and you visited Me."
> ### Matthew 25:34-36

Underline the reasons we're told to give in these verses.

Based on your study of these three Scriptures, what's one way God may be calling you to give in obedience to Him?

GIVING RECOGNIZES GOD'S OWNERSHIP. Giving comes back to the first question we explored together in this Bible study: Who owns it? Once we acknowledge God's ownership, giving is the natural response. Read the following verses that affirm God's ownership of all creation.

> The earth and everything in it,
> the world and its inhabitants,
> belong to the LORD.
> ### Psalm 24:1

Yours, LORD, is the greatness and the power and the glory and
the splendor and the majesty, for everything in the heavens and
on earth belongs to You. Yours, LORD, is the kingdom, and You are
exalted as head over all. Riches and honor come from You, and
You are the ruler of everything. Power and might are in Your hand,
and it is in Your hand to make great and to give strength to all.

1 Chronicles 29:11-12

**How does giving remind us of God's
ownership of our possessions?**

GIVING PROMISES REWARDS AND PLEASES GOD. I frequently see
people take this motive and twist it to serve their own ends. On one side
of the fence, we see prosperity teachers who tell us to give so that we can
get more for ourselves to keep. On the other side of the fence are teachers
who claim that giving with any expectation of reward is selfish and wrong.
Both of these perspectives distort this motive. God tells us that our generosity brings Him pleasure and that when He's pleased, He wants to reward
us. These rewards are primarily eternal in nature, and we don't know exactly
what they are, but we know that "God loves a cheerful giver" (2 Cor. 9:7)
and that He richly blesses those who honor Him with their resources.

**As you read the following verses,
underline the rewards for giving.**

Give to him, and don't have a stingy heart when you
give, and because of this the LORD your God will bless
you in all your work and in everything you do.

Deuteronomy 15:10

Give, and it will be given to you; a good measure—pressed down,
shaken together, and running over—will be poured into your lap.
For with the measure you use, it will be measured back to you.

Luke 6:38

I have received everything in full, and I have an abundance.
I am fully supplied, having received from Epaphroditus
what you provided—a fragrant offering, an acceptable
sacrifice, pleasing to God. And my God will supply all your
needs according to His riches in glory in Christ Jesus.
Now to our God and Father be glory forever and ever.

Philippians 4:18-20

What do you think an acceptable sacrifice to God looks like?

GIVING REVEALS GOD'S LOVE FOR US AND DEMONSTRATES OUR LOVE FOR OTHERS. God's generous love is unmatched; He gives us grace after grace through the saving work of Christ and through the ongoing power of the Holy Spirit. Because we're God's image bearers, our love for others is also demonstrated by radical generosity. God models generosity by giving us Jesus, along with "everything required for life and godliness" (2 Pet. 1:3). Notice what the following verses say about giving.

God loved the world in this way: He gave His One
and Only Son, so that everyone who believes
in Him will not perish but have eternal life.

John 3:16

Each person should do as he has decided in his heart—not
reluctantly or out of necessity, for God loves a cheerful giver.

2 Corinthians 9:7

**If God demonstrates His love by giving, how does
giving demonstrate our love for God and others?**

The underlying truth that's consistent in all these motives is the placement of our treasure. How do we determine where our treasure is? Our treasure is usually what we think about most, what we pursue, and what we want to obtain. Matthew 6:21 says, "Where your treasure is, there your heart will be also." Jesus' statement implies that our hearts follow the things on which we spend money. Let's look at two people in the Bible who had their treasures in two different places.

Read Mark 12:41-44 and Luke 12:16-21. Which of these two people do you feel sorry for? Which one inspires you?

The widow understood something very important: eternity is much more important than today. She was just like the man described in Matthew 13:44 who discovered a treasure buried in a field and in his joy sold everything he had and bought the field. This man did the same thing the woman did: he gave everything he had in order to gain the kingdom of heaven. We often think this man prospered in this world because he got a treasure in a field, and we miss the fact that he's an example of radical generosity. His treasure wasn't material riches but the kingdom of God. It wasn't a make-believe treasure but a real, tangible treasure worth everything he owned. He gave all he had in anticipation of eternity.

Giving breaks the power of money in our lives. The kingdom of heaven is worth far more than anything we own. As Jim Elliot famously said, "He is no fool who gives what he cannot keep to gain what he cannot lose."[1]

Where is this tension between earth and eternity most evident in your life today?

What do you need to give up to gain what you can't lose?

Spend a few minutes thanking God for His promise of eternity to those who love Him. Ask Him to help you view eternity in an appropriate light and see it as the priceless treasure it is.

1. Jim Elliot, as quoted in Elisabeth Elliot, *Through Gates of Spendor* (Wheaton: IL: Tyndale, 1981), 172.

reflect

In his book *Seeds of Hope* Henri Nouwen wrote:

> Our lives as we live them seem like lives that anticipate
> questions that never will be asked. It seems as if we are getting
> ourselves ready for the question "How much did you earn
> during your lifetime?" or "How many friends did you make?"
> or "How much progress did you make in your career?" or
> "How much influence did you have on people?" or "How many
> books did you write?" or "How many conversions did you
> make?" Were any of these to be the question Christ will ask
> when he comes again in glory, many of us in North America
> could approach the judgment day with great confidence.
>
> But nobody is going to hear any of these questions. The question
> we all are going to face is the question we are least prepared for.
> It is the question: "What have you done for the least of mine?" ...
>
> As long as there are strangers; hungry, naked, and sick people;
> prisoners, refugees, and slaves; people who are handicapped
> physically, mentally, or emotionally; people without work, a home,
> or a piece of land, there will be that haunting question from the
> throne of judgment: "What have you done for the least of mine?"[1]

Henri Nouwen

This quotation always convicts me. I have to ask myself on a regular basis whether I believe God gave me money so that I could raise my standard of living or my standard of giving. God may have given me an increase to enjoy it and to enhance my lifestyle, but it's very dangerous for me to assume that's automatically the case. If I'm faithful with what He's given me, I should expect Him to give me more to sow into His kingdom. David Platt said it well: "There is never going to come a day when I stand before God and he looks at me and says, 'I wish you would have kept more for yourself.' "[2]

Philippians 3:18-20 is a great reminder of this truth:

I have often told you, and now say again with tears, that many live as enemies of the cross of Christ. Their end is destruction; their god is their stomach; their glory is in their shame. They are focused on earthly things, but our citizenship is in heaven, from which we also eagerly wait for a Savior, the Lord Jesus Christ.

Philippians 3:18-20

How does money tempt you to find your god or your glory apart from God?

This lesson will challenge us to think about the amount of money we're giving to the Lord. I want to caution at the start that God designed giving and generosity to give us means of acknowledging His ownership and of breaking free from the love of money. Anytime people begin talking about how much to give, the opportunity arises for giving to become a legalistic and meaningless act that borders on the pharisaical. The trap is to quit believing God owns it all and to think only a certain percentage is His.

Every dollar we have represents an opportunity to bring glory to God. Every dollar we receive presents an opportunity to ask, "What's the best and most God-honoring use of this money? Would it best be used for the needs of my church? To buy dinner for my neighbors who are far from God? To take a vacation with my family and deepen our relationships?" The key in all these decisions lies in where our hearts are. Remember that God doesn't need our money, but He wants our hearts. He isn't measuring us by our money; rather, He's freeing us to serve Him and to bless others through our money.

How much do you think God requires you to give? Be honest and don't come back and change your answer at the end of this study.

What percentage of their money do you think the Israelites were required to give in the Old Testament? Select your answer.

0%   10%   18.5%   23.3%   More than 25%

In Deuteronomy Moses gave the Israelites guidelines for their required tithes (the word *tithe* simply means *a tenth).* There were three required tithes and multiple freewill offerings. The first tithe was for the yearly firstfruits of produce or flocks. This is what we typically think of as the tithe, or the 10-percent offering. The second tithe was the yearly firstfruits tithe that was to be eaten as a celebration. That's right; the Israelites were told to throw a party, using 10 percent of their income! That must have been quite a party. The final tithe, required only every third year, went to a local storehouse to care for sojourners, orphans, and widows.

If you're counting, the required tithes in the Old Testament added up to 23.3 per-cent of income. That didn't include various freewill offerings or the temple tax.

You may be thinking, *Those Old Testament offerings aren't relevant anymore. What about the New Testament?* The New Testament has plenty to say about giving, although it doesn't say a lot about tithing. Paul wrote:

> On the first day of the week, each of you is to set something aside and save in keeping with how he prospers, so that no collections will need to be made when I come.
> ## 1 Corinthians 16:2

This standard set forth seems to be based on how prosperous a person is. That would mean as your income goes up, so should your giving. Everyone should give according to what God has given to them.

Do you think the standard of giving in the New Testament is higher or lower than the standard in the Old Testament? Why?

When Jesus came, I don't think He lowered the bar for people who love Him. We certainly have grace and forgiveness if we fall short, but under grace our outpouring of gratitude naturally increases instead of decreasing.

One of the most important New Testament verses on giving is 2 Corinthians 9:7:

> Each person should do as he has decided in his heart—not reluctantly or out of necessity, for God loves a cheerful giver.
> ## 2 Corinthians 9:7

Do you consider yourself a cheerful giver?   Yes   No

**What would need to change for you
to be able to give cheerfully?**

Giving is a matter of the heart. The New Testament gives us grace and freedom, but that grace and freedom transform us into being more like Jesus, not less. When I discuss giving under the grace of the New Testament, I like to identify three standards of giving: should give, could give, and would give.

PROPORTIONATE GIVING: SHOULD GIVE

There are Christians who've never even considered tithing, and there are others who tithe to the penny. I'd like to free people at both ends of the spectrum, either from a position of resistance and shame or from a position of living by the letter of the law. Today I invite you to look at tithing through a fresh lens. As you consider where you fall on the should-give continuum, ask God to explode your view of giving, enabling you to see it as a powerful antidote to financial stress, materialism, and control.

Proportionate giving is the type of giving Paul taught in 2 Corinthians, where he commended the Macedonians for giving according to their ability (see 8:3). He had earlier encouraged the Corinthians to give as they had prospered (see 1 Cor. 16:2). This is what I refer to as proportionate giving. All of us have the ability to give at least a tithe. If God expected tithing from the poorest of the Israelites, surely that amount is within all our abilities. However, beware of the temptation to think of 10 percent of your income as God's and 90 percent as yours. Remember, it's all God's.

PLANNED GIVING: COULD GIVE

This giving simply represents an amount we could give if we were willing to give up something else. It may mean we plan to give up a vacation, a savings account, a lifestyle desire, or another possession. Intentional, planned giving is the closest most Americans will get to the sacrificial giving described in Luke 21:4 and 2 Corinthians 8:2-4.

Fill in this sentence: I could give

_____ if _____.

Imagine the possibilities. We could bless the world in so many ways if we took the time to dream and then act.

PRECOMMITTED GIVING: WOULD GIVE

This type of giving is faith giving. We commit ourselves to giving if the Lord provides us the means to do it. For instance, you may say if God gives you an extra one thousand dollars, you'll give it to a certain missions organization. Because you don't have that money available or don't feel called to give from your surplus, you precommit to giving something specific away if God provides you a way to do it. It's a great opportunity to dream big and then step out in faith when the Lord provides.

Take time to prayerfully think about your giving at these three levels. Then fill out the following chart.

GIVING PLEDGE

Recognizing that God wants me to be a good steward of His resources and use them for His purposes, I make the following giving pledge for the coming year.

	AMOUNT
What I should give:	$
What I could give by making a sacrifice in the following area:	$
What I would give if God blessed me with this amount:	$
I WILL GIVE:	$

SIGNED   DATE

Spend time in prayer, asking God to give you wisdom for the amount He wants you to give and where He wants you to give.

1. Henri Nouwen, *Seeds of Hope,* ed. Robert Durback (New York: Doubleday, 1997), 241–42.
2. David Platt, *Radical* (Colorado Springs: Multnomah, 2010), 123.

apply

As you begin to give regularly and recognize that God owns it all, I believe you'll see how absurd it is to accumulate more and more of God's resources, only to offer a simple "Thank You" in return. Giving with a Kingdom focus is a joyous journey, one I'm positive you won't regret. The opportunity to exercise faith when you begin to give generously is exciting, and I don't want you to miss it. Consider these thoughts by two of my favorite authors:

I do not believe one can settle how much we ought to give. I am afraid the only safe rule is to give more than we can spare.[1]

C. S. Lewis

Never be diplomatic and careful with the treasure God gives you.[2]

Oswald Chambers

Record ways you can take the truths from these two quotations and incorporate them into your finances.

I can't overemphasize the tremendous joy that comes from giving, especially when it's connected to the Kingdom and the missional work of the church. God created giving for our benefit. He doesn't need us to give Him anything, but He wants us to give Him everything.

How can you step out of your comfort zone during the next week and give generously to somebody else?

Consider the following modern-day paraphrase of the rich-fool passage in Luke 12:13-21.

> Someone in the crowd said to him, "Teacher, tell my boss to pay the full year-end performance bonus he promised me." But he said to him, "Man, who made me a judge or arbitrator over you?" And he said to them, "Take care, and be on your guard against all covetousness, for one's life does not consist in the abundance of his possessions." And he told them a parable, saying, "The stock options belonging to a manager vested after a major run-up in share price, and he thought to himself, 'What shall I do, for I already have enough saved to send my kids to college, my house is paid off, and I already max out my 401k every year!' And he said, 'I will do this: I will open an investment account and create a passive income portfolio, and I'll exercise my options and put the money there. And I will say to my soul, "Soul, you have a big enough portfolio to be financially independent; retire early, plan some vacations, play golf." ' But God said to him, 'Fool! This night your soul is required of you, and the portfolio you've built, what use will it be then?' So is the one who endlessly builds his net worth and is not rich toward God."[3]

**Put yourself in the place of the rich fool. What do
you notice about this paraphrase that's convicting?**

In a moment you'll spend some time solidifying and memorializing your convictions from this session. First let me give my personal convictions on the topics we've been discussing.

My personal convictions on giving:

1. Giving is an integral part of a maturing Christian's life.
2. Giving is commanded in Scripture, both for the benefit of the recipient and for the benefit of the giver.
3. It's wise to frequently, prayerfully consider the amount God is asking me to give.
4. Giving should be proportionate to my income and net worth.
5. Biblical giving is done regularly and cheerfully.
6. God doesn't need my money, but He wants my heart.
7. I give because giving reflects the nature of my Creator and demonstrates my love for Him.
8. God promises rewards for those who give. Whether those rewards are here or in heaven, they'll far exceed anything I could have bought with the money I gave away.

**Now record one or two personal convictions
about the topics we discussed this week.**

In what ways do you feel encouraged
by what you learned this week?

In what ways do you sense God moving you to
change, based on what you learned this week?

**Close your time in silence and prayer, listening to what
God is teaching you and asking Him for wisdom.**

The wisdom from above is first pure, then
peace-loving, gentle, compliant, full of mercy
and good fruits, without favoritism and hypocrisy.

James 3:17

1. C. S. Lewis, *Mere Christianity* (New York: Simon & Schuster, 1996), 82–83.
2. Oswald Chambers, *Utmost: Class Readings and Prayers from Oswald Chambers*
   (Crewe, UK: Oswald Chambers Publications Association, 2012), 62.
3. John Cortines and Gregory Baumer, *God and Money* (Carson, CA: Rose, 2016), 120-21.

WEEK 5

owe

start

Welcome to session 5 of God Owns It All. *Open the session with prayer. Then briefly discuss the following.*

What was one point that stood out to you as you completed last week's personal study?

What kind of questions are you seeing answered as you work through this study?

In this session we'll explore the Owe piece of the pie diagram. What one word comes to your mind when you think about debt or taxes?

Debt and taxes. If you had known what topic this session was going to address, would you have shown up? Admittedly, all of us would prefer not to owe debt or taxes.

This session will reveal what the Bible has to say about owing debt and owing taxes. We'll examine these questions: If everyone I know uses debt to purchase necessities and niceties, shouldn't I do it as well? Am I really expected to pay taxes with gratitude to a government that's wasteful or with which I disagree?

Read Luke 14:28 together. Then watch the video for session 5, in which Ron Blue offers a biblical perspective on owing debt and taxes.

watch

The rich rule over the poor,
and the borrower is a slave to the lender.
Proverbs 22:7

Biblical Principles of Borrowing

1. Anytime I borrow money, I am a slave to the lender.
2. I have to repay anything I borrow.
3. If you're going to borrow money, make sure you understand the true cost.
4. Don't presume upon the future.

Don't be one of those who enter agreements,
who put up security for loans.
If you have no money to pay,
even your bed will be taken from under you.
Proverbs 22:26-27

For which of you, wanting to build a tower, doesn't first
sit down and calculate the cost to see if he has enough to
complete it? Otherwise, after he has laid the foundation and
cannot finish it, all the onlookers will begin to make fun of him,
saying, "This man started to build and wasn't able to finish."
Luke 14:28-30

Come now, you who say, "Today or tomorrow we will travel to
such and such a city and spend a year there and do business
and make a profit." You don't even know what tomorrow
will bring—what your life will be! For you are like smoke that
appears for a little while, then vanishes. Instead, you should
say, "If the Lord wills, we will live and do this or that." But as
it is, you boast in your arrogance. All such boasting is evil.
James 4:13-16

Dangers of Debt

1. Economic
2. Spiritual
3. Psychological

The Magic of Compounding

1. The amount of money invested or borrowed
2. The interest rate earned or paid
3. The length of time

When you borrow money, you have the magic of compounding working against you as opposed to for you.

TRANSFERABLE CONCEPT

Getting in debt is easy. Getting out is a lot harder.

Credit cards are never a problem. It's the person who holds the credit card that is the problem.

Is It OK to Borrow Money?

1. The economic return must be greater than the economic cost.
2. Are you presuming upon the future when you take the debt out?
3. Am I denying God an opportunity to provide?
4. In borrowing money, the spouses should always be in agreement.

Credit-card debt and consumer debt never make sense economically.

Mortgage debt, investment debt, and student debt may make sense economically.

The Only Two Deductions that Make Economic Sense

1. Charitable
2. A retirement plan

discuss

In the video Ron explained that debt and taxes are symptoms of something else in our lives. Taxes are symptoms of income. Debt is often a symptom of spending more than we make. So, as with other uses of money, our issues with debt and taxes are really issues of our hearts.

Do you agree with Ron that financial issues are symptoms of heart issues? What have you experienced that causes you to agree or disagree with him?

What do you think your personal view of debt and taxes reveals about your heart today?

There are many types of debt, and there are many reasons for going into debt. Some so-called experts argue that certain types of debt are foolish not to use. Nevertheless, the Bible teaches that a borrower becomes a slave to the lender (see Prov. 22:7). Always.

What does it mean for a borrower to be a slave to the lender?

If the borrower becomes a slave to the lender, should debt ever be used?

Ron taught that while the Bible teaches that a borrower becomes a slave to the lender, it doesn't teach that borrowing money is a sin. It may be foolish or unwise to borrow money, but the Bible doesn't say it's a sin.

Ron proposed four biblical principles of borrowing that we can use to evaluate whether to take on debt.

Which principle do you find to be
most difficult to follow or to grasp?

What are some dangers inherent in presuming on the future?

Ron made the rather unorthodox statement that we should be thankful for the taxes we pay because they indicate that we have an income.

Respond to Ron's perspective of gratitude toward taxes.
How could you model gratitude as you pay your taxes?

Ron teaches that taxes are a stewardship opportunity. Our choice in paying taxes is either faithfulness or fraud. If God owns it all and He tells us to pay taxes to the government, that's what we should do (see Matt. 22:17-21).

How do you balance honoring God by paying taxes and holding
the government accountable for the ways it spends tax revenue?

In closing, ask God to help you see any heart issues you have with respect to debt and taxes.

study

In 1979, after much prayer and wise counsel, I decided to leave full-time vocational ministry and start a financial-planning company. I thought it would be wise to obtain a line of credit from a bank in order to have cash on hand during the beginning stage of my new business. So I went to a bank and secured a $10,000 line of credit.

In my devotional times during the following weeks, I became uncomfortable with the idea of borrowing money to start my business. It felt hypocritical to start a business in debt when I intended to encourage my clients to avoid using debt. I became so convicted that I canceled the line of credit. This decision felt extremely risky because I had seven mouths to feed, no reliable source of income, and no clients. Nonetheless, I had found that it was best to obey when I sensed God's conviction.

One week after canceling the line of credit, I was meeting with some of the staff at a major international corporation and telling them about my new venture. They asked me if I would consider creating a financial-training seminar and delivering it to their employees four times during the next year. Eager for any opportunity, I said yes. When they asked me how much I would charge for that seminar, I was at a loss. I hadn't thought about the charge for the work, so I asked them how much they would pay. (I know; not the best negotiation tactic.)

They said they would pay me $6,000 up front (right away) to develop the seminar and $1,000 for each time I taught it. That added up to $10,000, the exact amount of the line of credit I had canceled. I'm convinced that if I hadn't given up my line of credit, I never would have gotten the opportunity to develop the seminar and, even if I had, I wouldn't have seen it as God's provision. I felt as if God were telling me, "I know what you need. Trust Me."

Before we explore what the Bible has to say about debt, I want to start with some encouragement. No matter who you are, how much debt you have, or what decisions you've made in the past, your debt and past decisions don't define who you are. Debt can be eliminated by making a choice to do so and living within the confines of biblical principles. God is a God of forgiveness and redemption. No matter what your situation is, remember that there's hope. God loves you no matter what. Your debt doesn't define you, but it can confine you. So let's find out what God has to say about debt and then equip you with some tools to escape its bondage.

We'll start with the foundational understanding that if you can avoid using debt, you should. There are many dangers to having debt—emotional, spiritual, and psychological—but I want to explore two specific spiritual dangers of debt.

DEBT ALWAYS PRESUMES UPON THE FUTURE. Read the following scriptural warning:

> Come now, you who say, "Today or tomorrow we will travel to such and such a city and spend a year there and do business and make a profit." You don't even know what tomorrow will bring—what your life will be! For you are like smoke that appears for a little while, then vanishes. Instead, you should say, "If the Lord wills, we will live and do this or that." But as it is, you boast in your arrogance. All such boasting is evil.
>
> James 4:13-16

How does this passage say we tend to approach the future?

What are some dangerous presumptions you make about the future when you acquire debt?

No matter who you are, if you have debt, you presume that you'll have the means to pay it off in the future. Nobody knows the future but God. Debt is dangerous because it puts your confidence in the future in the place of God.

DEBT MAY DENY GOD AN OPPORTUNITY TO WORK. The story at the beginning of this lesson is a perfect example of how debt can deny God an opportunity to work. If I had relied on the bank for the line of credit, I wouldn't have experienced God's provision in the same way and may not have experienced it at all. We experience joy when we see God work.

Read the following verses and underline the truths about God or His provision.

"My thoughts are not your thoughts,
and your ways are not My ways."
This is the LORD's declaration.
"For as heaven is higher than earth,
so My ways are higher than your ways,
and My thoughts than your thoughts."
Isaiah 55:8-9

Consider the ravens: They don't sow or reap; they
don't have a storeroom or a barn; yet God feeds them.
Aren't you worth much more than the birds?
Luke 12:24

Don't worry, saying, "What will we eat?" or "What will we drink?"
or "What will we wear?" For the idolaters eagerly seek all these
things, and your heavenly Father knows that you need them.
Matthew 6:31-32

Do you have more faith in the bank or in God to provide for you?

Why is it tempting to put your faith in a bank?

Having a good understanding of the spiritual dangers of debt is helpful for internalizing and understanding the principle you learned in week 2:

Avoid debt, because debt always mortgages the future.

What do I mean by saying debt mortgages the future? Simply put, if I take on debt today, I precommit the way I'll spend certain dollars in the future. For instance, if I take out a loan to buy a car and have a $350 monthly payment for three years, I've already determined the way I'm going to spend $350 of my monthly income for the next three years. I've thus limited my flexibility by giving a third party (the lender) the right to demand that I spend that $350 a certain way each month.

Jesus gave some advice about predetermining our future:

> He told them a parable: "A rich man's land was very productive. He thought to himself, 'What should I do, since I don't have anywhere to store my crops? I will do this,' he said. 'I'll tear down my barns and build bigger ones and store all my grain and my goods there. Then I'll say to myself, "You have many goods stored up for many years. Take it easy; eat, drink, and enjoy yourself." ' But God said to him, 'You fool! This very night your life is demanded of you. And the things you have prepared—whose will they be?' That's how it is with the one who stores up treasure for himself and is not rich toward God."
> Luke 12:16-21

What mistake did this rich man make about the future?

How can you compare taking on debt to buy something you don't have the cash to pay for now with the mistake that the rich man made in this parable?

Only God knows the future. When we take on substantial amounts of debt, we remove from our lives the flexibility we need to respond quickly to God's direction. Suppose you had $25,000 of credit-card debt when you sensed God was calling you to become a missionary in the Philippines. You couldn't follow that call until you paid off your debts at home, because your future had been mortgaged.

This brings us to the next huge concept for debt: our relationship with our lenders. Read some ways the Bible addresses this subject:

The rich rule over the poor,
and the borrower is a slave to the lender.
Proverbs 22:7

Don't be one of those who enter agreements,
who put up security for loans.
If you have no money to pay,
even your bed will be taken from under you.
Proverbs 22:26-27

**What are some implications you've experienced
of being a slave to a lender?**

**Are you willing to fully submit to debt as your master,
or would you rather serve someone or something else?**

Admittedly, there are many different reasons for going into debt, some of them very valid. To help you sift through the confusion, I've developed four questions to ask before taking on debt. If you can't answer all these questions yes, then you shouldn't take on that debt.

1. Is the economic return greater than the economic cost?
2. Is there a guaranteed way to repay the loan?
3. Will this debt avoid the spiritual dangers of debt?
4. Are my spouse and I in agreement about this debt?

Credit-card debt and car debt are two of the most common forms of debt. These debts almost always fail the first question above. This type of debt is usually a symptom of spending more than we make. In an attempt to improve our lifestyle, we end up mortgaging our future.

I know paying cash for a car is countercultural, but it never makes economic sense to finance the purchase of a car. Generally speaking, people usually have the ability to save in order to buy a cheap car for the short term and then save for a better car for the long term. The wise decision here is delayed gratification over instant gratification.

In the next lesson we'll explore the true cost of debt. For now it's important to understand that the spiritual and emotional cost of debt can be enormous. Being a slave to a lender is always confining. Until we experience life without the bondage of debt, it's impossible for us to understand how much of a chain that debt is. We can't truly understand freedom until we've actually been free.

This following Scriptures say it well:

> Do not owe anyone anything, except to love one another,
> for the one who loves another has fulfilled the law.
> Romans 13:8

> Watch out and be on guard against all greed because
> one's life is not in the abundance of his possessions.
> Luke 12:15

**Is anything you own worth more than your
future or more than honoring God?**

**Does your life reflect your answer to that question? If not,
what changes do you need to make so that it does?**

Spend a few minutes asking God to show you ways He's bigger than all your earthly wants and desires. Ask Him to help you move past the idea that more stuff and more debt can satisfy the longings of your heart.

reflect

Imagine for a moment that you're holding a tube of toothpaste. Think about how easy it is to squeeze out the toothpaste. Now imagine that you empty a full tube of toothpaste onto your bathroom counter. Generally speaking, that task wouldn't have been very difficult. But now picture yourself trying to put the toothpaste from your counter back into the tube. If you've never tried to do this, I'll tell you that it's nearly impossible. It's also extremely messy!

I like to think of debt that way. It's so easy to spend money but so hard to repay it (not to mention messy). It seems that everywhere you go, somebody wants to offer you a new credit card. Why? It's really very simple: it's extremely lucrative for companies when you buy with credit instead of cash. Every time you use credit for a purchase, someone earns a fee and probably interest. Nobody offers you credit because they like you or think you need an advantage. They offer you credit so that they can make money.

Once you have credit, it's easy to believe you got that credit only because people smarter than you believe you'll be able to repay it. Therefore, you use it, and the debt starts adding up. Unfortunately, your ability to repay debt has very little to do with a credit-card company's decision to provide you with credit. They actually don't want you to repay your debts in a timely fashion. The quicker you repay your debts, the less money they make.

The whole system is designed to encourage you to have debt and lots of it. After all, that's what keeps the economy healthy, right?

Let's take some time to understand how costly debt really is and why instead of enhancing your lifestyle, it actually degrades your lifestyle in the long term.

The true cost of debt can't be fully understood without a basic understanding of the magic of compounding, a financial concept so powerful that Albert Einstein once called it the eighth wonder of the world. He said, "He who understands it, earns it. ... He who doesn't, pays it."[1]

Compounding is the process of earning interest on the interest already applied to the principal. For example, if you owe $10 at 10 percent interest, after one year you'll owe $1 of interest and $10 of principal. If you make no payments, you'll then owe $11, and all $11 will be charged interest. You're now paying interest on interest. This concept works for the lender or investor and against the borrower.

Let's look at an example of compound interest working against you. In 2015 the average credit-card debt was $15,762.[2] If you assume an 18 percent interest rate, the minimum amount the credit-card company *requires* you to pay is approximately $240 a month. If you make only the minimum payment, it will take nearly 21 years to repay this debt, and you'll pay over $44,000 in interest. The total cost of that $15,000 will be approximately $59,000. Not only does that mean you paid almost four times the cost of the initial debt, but you were also unable to use that $44,000 to do anything else; you've cost yourself a tremendous amount of flexibility.

> **Knowing that using credit to buy something could make an item cost up to four times its actual value, why do you think credit is so tempting for people to use?**

I mentioned earlier that not only does compounding work against you when you borrow money, but you ultimately end up degrading the quality of your future lifestyle when you borrow money to fund your present lifestyle. In my experience most people go into debt to buy something they otherwise couldn't have bought. The most common reason people do this is to increase their lifestyle. Perhaps you think if you can buy the nice thing you want now, you'll have increased your lifestyle. That may be true for the short term, but let me give you an example of how this scenario plays out in the long term.

Assume I overspend by $1,000 every year for 10 years and use debt to fund that extra spending. This debt is charging interest at 10 percent a year. After 10 years I decide I want to get out of debt. To do this, I have to take these steps.

1. Quit overspending by $1,000 each year.
2. Come up with money to repay the money I borrowed plus the interest that has accumulated over time.

After 10 years I'll owe $10,000 to the lender, and that $10,000 will generate interest. To pay it off will require me to reduce my lifestyle by $3,000. That's $2,000 to repay principal and interest and $1,000 as a result of not over-spending any longer. This repayment will reduce the quality of my lifestyle for the next 10 years. Suddenly this seems like a really bad idea! The following chart depicts this concept.

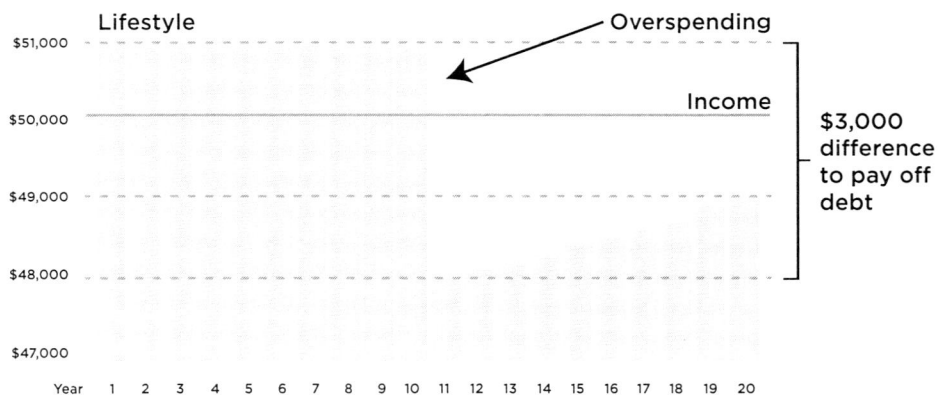

How have you seen this concept play itself out in your life?

In what ways is borrowing money to fund lifestyle desires tempting to you? Spend some time examining specific ways, why it's tempting, and what this communicates about your heart.

The hard truth is that we always have to make sacrifices in our lives to get out of debt. We may also have to make sacrifices to stay out of debt. This is a hard journey, but it's amazingly worth it.

I once hired a young woman who had just graduated from college. She was the first in her family to do so. Before going to college, she set a goal to graduate with $15,000 of debt or less. To do this, she had to apply for financial aid, work a few jobs, live a modest lifestyle, and plan ahead. With her goal in mind, she managed to make it through college just above her goal. She graduated with about $16,000 in debt.

That's a great story, but it gets better. Once she graduated, she set a goal to repay the debt within one year. Again, she had to make some sacrifices in how much she worked, where she lived, what kind of car she drove, and how much entertainment she could afford. By working hard, she paid off her college debt in about 10 months. She was determined to get out of debt, but she also understood that her desire required sacrifices. She demonstrated the principle we talked about in week 2:

Financial maturity is being able to give up today's desires for future benefits.

Here are the steps to take if you're in debt and want to get out.

1. Decide you'll no longer go into debt.
2. List all your debts, from the smallest to the largest, on the table below. Exclude home mortgage for now.
3. Reduce all your monthly expenses to the minimum.
4. Use all available excess cash to repay the smallest debt.
5. After you've paid off the smallest debt, apply all the money you were using to pay off that debt to the next smallest debt.
6. Continue until all your debt is repaid.

Lender's Name	Principal Balance	Minimum Payment
1.	$	$
2.	$	$
3.	$	$
4.	$	$
5.	$	$
6.	$	$
7.	$	$
8.	$	$

Here's a simple example. Suppose you owed $1,000 to Visa and $2,000 to MasterCard. Each debt has a minimum payment of $200. Assume you have $500 available for debt repayment. You would begin by paying $300 on the Visa bill each month, with $200 still going to MasterCard. Once you've repaid Visa, you would apply all $500 to the MasterCard bill. Soon both debts would be repaid.

Take a few minutes to ask God to give you wisdom and perseverance to pay off any debt you have. If you're married, talk and pray with your spouse this week about committing to a debt-repayment plan together.

1. Albert Einstein, *Quotes on Finance* [online, cited 5 May 2016]. Available from the Internet: *quotesonfinance.com*.
2. Erin El Issa, "2015 American Household Credit Card Debt Study," *Nerdwallet* [online, cited 5 May 2016]. Available from the Internet: *nerdwallet.com*.

apply

We're all products of our culture. Many times we go along with what appears to be a good idea in our culture, only to look back years later and realize how foolish we were. In a similar way, I believe one day we'll look back at the debt we've accumulated individually and as a society and wonder how we could ever have been so foolish. A debt-heavy lifestyle almost always stems from a lack of contentment with the lifestyle God has given us at the time. This is as much a spiritual problem as it is an education problem.

**What are some things you once believed were
true or good ideas that you laugh about today?**

All of us know that having too much debt is a bad idea, but for some reason we don't put that knowledge into practice. The definition of *stupidity* is *doing the same thing over and over again while expecting a different result.* Let's not be foolish or stupid when it comes to debt. Admit the mistakes of the past and then make a better future by following God's Word in the way we manage money.

Let's be clear on the Bible does and doesn't say about debt:

- The Bible *doesn't* say it's a sin to borrow or loan money.
- The Bible *doesn't* say it's wise to borrow or loan.
- The Bible *doesn't* say God will bail you out of debt.
- The Bible *doesn't* say debt is an exercise of faith.
- The Bible *does* say it's wrong not to repay debts (see Ps. 37:21).
- The Bible *does* say it's foolish to put yourself in a surety situation (see Prov. 11:15).

Scripture reminds us:

Jesus Christ is the same yesterday, today, and forever.
Hebrews 13:8

If you know God is the same yesterday, today, and tomorrow, what are some ways you can confidently follow His principles on debt and taxes, trusting that they'll lead you to a more secure financial future?

A man I'm fortunate to call a friend lived these principles to a level that's virtually unheard of anywhere. This friend's name is Ralph Meloon. His father founded the Correct Craft boat company, the maker of Ski Nautique ski boats. When Ralph and his brother were running the company, the U.S. government placed a large order of assault boats for use in the Korean War. Because a government inspector was looking for a bribe and the Meloons refused to pay, a number of the boats were rejected for not meeting specifications.

As a result of this rejection and other related incidents, the Meloons' company was forced to file for bankruptcy protection. They came out of bankruptcy with no legal obligation to repay any of their creditors, and 80 percent of their debt was canceled. Consequently, 228 creditors didn't receive full payment of the debts owed to them.

Feeling that failing to repay their debts would violate the teachings of the Bible, Ralph and his brother committed to repay all their debts, despite being under no legal obligation to do so. Over the next 18 years they scrapped and clawed, eventually tracking down all their creditors and repaying every cent they owed. To do this cost them nearly twice what was owed and required them to make amazing sacrifices in the way they lived. Ralph, his wife, and their three kids lived in a tent for 5½ years during this time. Repaying debt required them to give up their present security. In their minds, though, not to repay their debt would be disobedient to God.

Ralph's family's story is one of great sacrifice and generosity. I have great affection for Ralph and believe he's a very good man. What concerns me most about this story is that it's not the norm. Why isn't this the story of every Christian who goes through bankruptcy? Where's the character that Ralph exhibited? Unfortunately, it's the exception and not the rule. Ralph was blessed by his experience. Through the struggle of repaying his debts, he found great joy and reliance on Christ. Too often we want to run from trouble instead of growing through it. I pray that believers will make Ralph's story common when they face financial adversity.

Here are my personal convictions on this week's topics:

1. Borrowing isn't a sin.
2. Borrowing may deny God an opportunity to work.
3. Borrowing always presumes upon the future.
4. Debt is the inability to repay amounts borrowed on a timely basis.
5. Debt is almost always a symptom of spiritual problems.
6. Consumptive borrowing will sentence me to a reduced lifestyle in the future and will limit financial flexibility and future financial freedom.
7. Getting into debt is much easier than getting out of debt.
8. Using debt to fund an enhanced lifestyle today will condemn me to a reduced quality of life tomorrow.
9. Husband and wife must be in perfect agreement about borrowing.
10. Income taxes should never be the source of cash-flow problems. They may be a symptom of other issues, such as lifestyle, debt, or poor planning.
11. The tax tail should never wag the family dog. That is, you should never allow the tax consequences of a decision to be the controlling factor in making decisions about your finances.
12. Income taxes are an indicator of God's blessings and should be paid with a spirit of thankfulness.

Record one or two personal convictions
from the topics we discussed this week.

In what ways do you feel encouraged
by what you learned this week?

How do you sense God moving you to change,
based on what you learned this week?

*Close your time in silence and prayer, listening to what God is teaching you
and asking Him for wisdom.*

The wisdom from above is first pure, then
peace-loving, gentle, compliant, full of mercy
and good fruits, without favoritism and hypocrisy.

James 3:17

WEEK 6

grow

start

Welcome to session 6, the final session of God Owns It All. *Open the session with prayer. Then briefly discuss the following.*

What was one point that stood out to you as you completed last week's personal study?

What's the greatest risk to you or your faith in using debt?

In this session we'll explore the Grow piece of the pie diagram. In one word how would you describe the importance of saving for the future?

Excess cash flow and margin are the cornerstones of any successful financial plan. Without extra money it's impossible to meet long-term goals and objectives. This session explores Grow, the piece of the pie diagram we can use to meet those long-term goals.

In order to grow and balance the rest of our pie, we need the tools and techniques to get there. Goal setting and decision making are the tools that can get us where we want to be and where God is calling us to go. This final session will encourage us to move toward financial maturity as we seek God's wisdom about our resources.

Read Philippians 3:12-14 together. Then watch the video for session 6, in which Ron Blue discusses the Grow piece of the pie, goal setting, and decision making.

watch

The less you owe, the more you can grow.

TRANSFERABLE CONCEPT

You need to plan for financial margin because
the unexpected is always going to occur.

Typical Prioritization of Spending

1. Live
2. Owe debt
3. Owe taxes
4. Grow
5. Give

Biblical Prioritization of Spending

1. Give
2. Grow
3. Owe debt
4. Owe taxes
5. Live

The longer term the perspective, the better the decision I can make today.

Giving up today's desires for future benefits is necessary because you want the magic of compounding working for you as opposed to against you.

The Magic of Compounding

A little bit over a long time frame becomes a lot in the long term.

When you've shifted from owing to growing, you need to let the magic of compounding work for you over a long time frame.

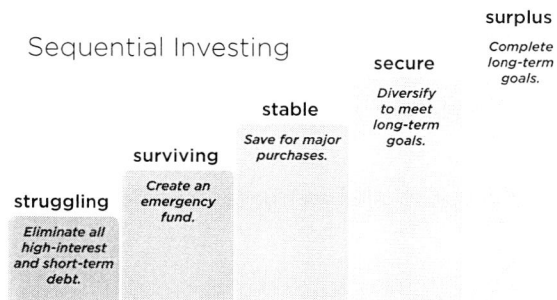

Sequential Investing

					surplus
				secure	Complete long-term goals.
			stable	Diversify to meet long-term goals.	
	surviving	Save for major purchases.		
struggling	Create an emergency fund.			
Eliminate all high-interest and short-term debt.				

Living within your income is the only way you move from level to level.

Nehemiah's Steps for Goal Setting

1. Identified with the problem
2. Prayed specifically
3. Experienced fear
4. Surveyed the situation
5. Set a goal
6. Relied on God

The goal will always be accomplished if it's a goal that God put in my heart, and God will get all of the glory.

Look at the sequential-investing chart, pray through it, set a goal, trust God for the results, and give Him the glory when it's accomplished.

Traps in Making Decisions

1. The binary trap: Should I do this or not?
2. The intuitive trap: I felt it was the right decision.
3. The voting trap: gathering opinions about the decision

Compare the alternatives to our goals, priorities, or objectives, not to one another.

discuss

The Bible tells us that the most productive uses of money are giving and saving, the required uses of money are debt and taxes, and what's left goes to our lifestyle. Unfortunately, many of us let our priorities for using money happen to us instead of determining our priorities in advance and allocating our resources accordingly.

How do you prioritize your uses of money?

How can ordering your use of money in accordance with the Bible provide freedom and contentment in your finances?

What's the hardest challenge for you in determining lifestyle spending only after all other areas are funded?

Ron told two stories about the magic of compounding. Each story was astounding because the world wouldn't ordinarily view either person as capable of accumulating wealth.

What's most amazing to you about these stories?

How can you cement in your mind and habits the fact that saving a little over a long time is the only sure way to reach your financial goals?

We can all place ourselves somewhere on the sequential-investing chart that Ron presented. The only way to move from one level to the next is to spend less than we earn and do it for a long period of time.

Should everyone have a goal of getting to the top step (surplus) of the sequential-investing chart? Why or why not?

Why would it be important to have goals or predetermined
action steps as you move from one level to the next?
What would be the potential danger of not doing so?

Ron used the biblical account of Nehemiah and the rebuilding of the wall
in Jerusalem to illustrate what it means to set a faith goal. The key question
Nehemiah asked was "God, what do You want me to do?"

Have you ever experienced fear in undertaking a task or a
goal you felt God leading you to do? Tell the group about it.

Why do God-given goals tend to lead us into fear?

Why is that a good thing?

Decision making is the final tool Ron taught in this session. This tool helps
us make confident decisions by bringing together all the principles and
concepts we've learned in this study.

Which of the decision-making traps that Ron described
have you experienced in your past decisions?

Describe a time when you made what turned out to be a
bad decision but learned and grew through that decision.

*In closing, ask God to help you move toward financial maturity in all phases
of your life. Ask Him to give you the willingness to forgo the desires of today
for the benefits of tomorrow and all eternity.*

study

For each of the following questions, jot down
the first thing that comes to your mind.

What percentage of your income should you save?

Does saving demonstrate a lack of faith?

Is failing to save irresponsible?

What's the number one reason you should save?

I once read a story about a man named Joe Temeczko, an immigrant from Poland who had survived internment at multiple prisoner-of-war camps during World War II. He moved to the United States in the 1950s and took a job cleaning the Statue of Liberty. Eventually, he moved to Minneapolis, where he did odd jobs as a carpenter, handyman, and roofer. Neighbors often saw him collecting discarded items around his neighborhood that he restored and sold. Mr. Temeczko was a regular at the local shelters where he went to get free food, and he often read newspapers inside stores so that he wouldn't have to pay for them. He lived an extremely frugal life.

Mr. Temeczko died of a heart attack at age 86 doing work around his house. To everyone's surprise, he left behind a $1.4 million bank account, which was given to the city of New York. This man worked hard, endured a tremendous amount of hardship, and somehow managed to save a tremendous amount of money.

I have to be honest, though. When I first read this story, I was unsure of whether to use it as an example of diligent saving or as a warning against harboring a fear of the future. I've come to the conclusion that it's both. On one hand, this story demonstrates the power of giving up the desires of the present for the benefit of the future. On the other hand, it demonstrates that a fear of loss and the future can overwhelm the ability to enjoy God's blessings.

This is the struggle all of us must deal with when we think about the Grow piece of the pie, and it brings to light the question "How much is enough?" Am I hoarding money in fear of the future and relying on myself, or am I responsibly saving for the needs of myself and my family? These are financially wise questions that we ought to wrestle with. Let's turn to Scripture:

Go to the ant, you slacker!
Observe its ways and become wise.
Without leader, administrator, or ruler,
it prepares its provisions in summer;
it gathers its food during harvest.
Proverbs 6:6-8

Precious treasure and oil are in the dwelling of a wise person,
but a foolish man consumes them.
Proverbs 21:20

Which of you, wanting to build a tower, doesn't first sit down and calculate the cost to see if he has enough to complete it? Otherwise, after he has laid the foundation and cannot finish it, all the onlookers will begin to make fun of him, saying, "This man started to build and wasn't able to finish."
Luke 14:28-30

**Summarize three points from these passages
about the importance of saving.**

1. _____

2. _____

3. _____

Like the ant, we need to save for the future. Saving isn't the same for everyone, because God has given us all different goals and objectives. Therefore, the practice of saving requires prayerful consideration of what God is asking us to keep for the future. With that in mind, let's explore the difference between saving and hoarding.

As you read the following parable, underline the man's mistake.

"I'll tear down my barns and build bigger ones and store all my grain and my goods there. Then I'll say to myself, 'You have many goods stored up for many years. Take it easy; eat, drink, and enjoy yourself.' " But God said to him, "You fool! This very night your life is demanded of you. And the things you have prepared—whose will they be?" That's how it is with the one who stores up treasure for himself and is not rich toward God.

Luke 12:18-21

The Bible helps us further distinguish between saving and hoarding:

Anyone trusting in his riches will fall,
but the righteous will flourish like foliage.

Proverbs 11:28

If anyone does not provide for his own, that is his own household, he has denied the faith and is worse than an unbeliever.

1 Timothy 5:8

Thinking we'll find life in what we possess is the key to understanding the fine line between saving and hoarding. When our hearts are moved by how much we have, whether in material things or in the size of our bank accounts, instead of by the One who has saved us, we're on dangerous ground. Randy Alcorn distinguishes between saving and hoarding this way: "Saving is a means of not presuming upon God. Hoarding is a means of replacing God."[1]

**Select the statement that best describes
your heart's posture in regard to saving.**

☐ I know I need to save but feel that I can't.
☐ I feel that saving is a lack of faith. I will trust God to provide.
☐ I hate spending money, so I save all I can and keep all I can.
☐ I'm afraid of what the future may hold, so I save everything.
☐ I trust God for the future but believe it's wise to save.
☐ I save some but don't think about it much.

Record on the heart what you want your heart's posture to be in regard to saving.

The key in this discussion is understanding where our hearts are. We must continually put all we have before God and ask Him what He wants us to do with it. It's all His anyway; we're His stewards. Our job is to inquire of Him what He wants us to do with His resources.

This inquiry leads us into the concept of setting faith goals. I love the saying "If you aim at nothing, you'll hit it every time." This means if we never set goals, we'll never know when we meet them.

Recall the definition of *stewardship* from week 1:

The use of God-given gifts and resources—such as time, talent, treasure, influence, and relationships—for the accomplishment of God-given goals and objectives

Underline the last part of that definition. If we don't know the goals and objectives God has for us, how can we apply our gifts and resources toward those ends? A faith goal, then, is an objective toward which we believe God wants us to move. It asks, "God, what are Your plans?" or it says, "God, I'm available—not necessarily able but available." Setting a faith goal could mean paying off debt, buying a new house, or going to the mission field.

Read the classic definition of *faith* from Hebrews:

Faith is the reality of what is hoped for, the proof of what is not seen. For our ancestors won God's approval by it. By faith we understand that the universe was created by God's command, so that what is seen has been made from things that are not visible.

Hebrews 11:1-3

How do you define *faith* in terms of your financial goals?

Perhaps you feel your financial situation is hopeless or your desires for the future are unattainable. How is God glorified when you seek His will in your finances and set goals that feel impossible to accomplish on your own?

Confining God to "realistic" expectations is a foolish idea. If you set only goals that are easy to accomplish, you lose the opportunity to see God come through.

Read these passages and answer the questions that follow.

Now to Him who is able to do above and beyond all that we ask or think according to the power that works in us.

Ephesians 3:20

Do not remember the past events,
pay no attention to things of old.
Look, I am about to do something new;
even now it is coming. Do you not see it?
Indeed, I will make a way in the wilderness,
rivers in the desert.

Isaiah 43:18-19

The LORD asked Abraham, "Why did Sarah laugh, saying,
'Can I really have a baby when I'm old?' Is anything
impossible for the LORD? At the appointed time I will come
back to you, and in about a year she will have a son."

Genesis 18:13-14

Which of the following best describes
God's ability to accomplish things?

☐ **God is confined to the laws of nature.**
☐ **God is unable to help me in my situation.**
☐ **God can do the impossible.**

What new thing can you imagine God doing in your life—
the God who's able to make a river in the desert?

When you set faith goals, don't focus on the past and don't focus on your present resources or limitations. Remember how big God is and trust that He's more than able. Finally, don't write your goals in concrete; write them in sand. Goals help you grow and increase your faith. They can change as God works in your life, heart, and character.

Remember that no goal is more spiritual than another as long as you're seeking God's guidance and pursuing what you believe God wants you to do. God delights in seeing you delight in watching Him move on your behalf.

Spend a few minutes asking God what He wants
you to do with your resources. How will you
act on your financial goals this week?

1. Randy C. Alcorn, *Money, Possessions, and Eternity* (Carol Stream, IL: Tyndale, 2003).

reflect

Imagine that a man and a woman began working in 1975 and retired in 2015. The woman invested $5,000 every year for the first 10 years of her working life. After that she invested nothing else. The man didn't invest anything during the first 10 years of his working life but then invested $5,000 every year for the next 30 years. Therefore, the woman invested a total of $50,000, and the man invested a total of $150,000. They both saved well, but who had more money at retirement?

Who had more on the date of retirement if each person was able to earn a 10 percent rate of return each year? Circle one.

The woman   The man

Who had more on the date of retirement if each person was able to earn an 8 percent rate of return each year? Circle one.

The woman   The man

Believe it or not, the woman had more money at retirement in both of these examples. In the first example the woman retired with $1,529,542, and the man retired with $904,717. In the second example the woman retired with $787,176, and the man retired with $611,729. As I said, both of these people did a good job of saving, but the woman was able to take advantage of the magic of compounding for a longer period of time. Even though she invested much less, that amount was able to grow for a longer period of time. That's the magic of compounding.

In week 5 we saw compounding working against us with debt. With savings compounding works for us. We should do everything we can to make compounding work for us, knowing both its danger and its power.

Understanding the concept of compounding allows us to see how we can progress on the sequential-investing chart.

On the following chart, mark three points: where you are now, where you think you need to be in order to freely serve God, and where you want to be. Number the points 1, 2, and 3.

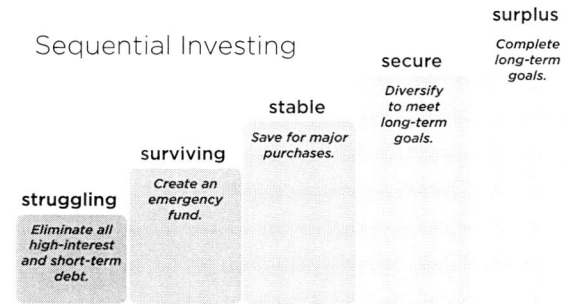

Explain why you answered the way you did and what step you need to take to get there.

It's very important to understand that going higher on the chart isn't always better. The purpose of this chart is simply to illustrate the point that you need to know where you are and where you're going. If you're struggling and you want to get to the stable or secure levels, you can develop a plan and set goals. Likewise, if you're in the surplus category and feel you have more than you need, you can make a plan to come back down the chart toward the secure or stable level.

I don't believe that God's plan is for all of us to be standing on the surplus step. God uses people at every one of these levels. That being said, I believe every Christian who's struggling or surviving can apply good financial wisdom to get to the stable category. Becoming stable frees you to follow God when He leads.

What do you need to do to move from the step you labeled as number 1 on the chart to the step you labeled as number 2?

In what ways will moving to the step you labeled as number 2 affect your daily life?

Have you ever run a marathon or thought about running a marathon? Me neither. I've never enjoyed running, and just the thought of running a marathon makes me feel tired. Although I don't know much about training for a marathon, I know this: if I want to run in a marathon, I need to start running. Can you imagine someone who never runs trying to run a marathon? It might actually kill them. The only way to train for a marathon is to start running short distances. Over time you gradually increase the distance you run, and eventually, after months of hard work, you're prepared to run a marathon.

Our financial lives are very similar to training for a marathon. We can't move from being deep in debt to having a surplus by simply changing behavior in one day. It takes time. If we want to move from one step to another step on the sequential-investing chart, it takes discipline and time. Just as we can't expect to be an Olympic-level marathon runner by simply buying running shoes, we can't expect to get our finances in order by simply doing a Bible study or taking a class. We must put into practice what we've learned, and somebody must hold us accountable.

> **Make a list of trusted people in your life or resources that can help keep you accountable in your finances.**

> **Using the previous illustration of the marathon, describe the training you may want to build into your life to make it easier to move from one step on the chart to the next.**

We'll end this lesson by revisiting the pie diagram. If we take all the principles and concepts we've learned these past six weeks and apply them to our pie diagrams, we see some pretty dramatic results. Let's assume your pie diagram looks like this:

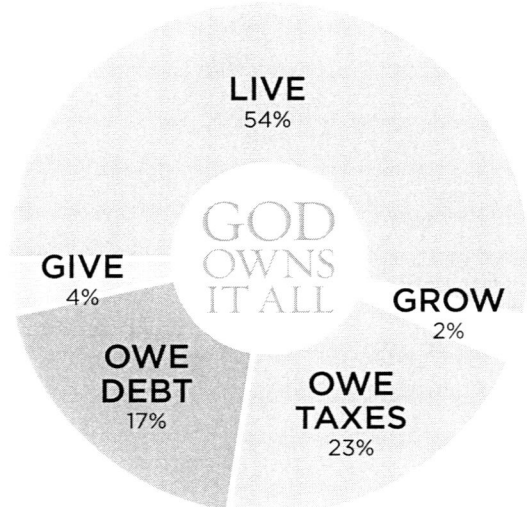

Through prayer and planning you decide you want to pay off all your debt, increase your giving to 12 percent, and increase your savings to 10 percent. If you did all those things, your pie would look like this:

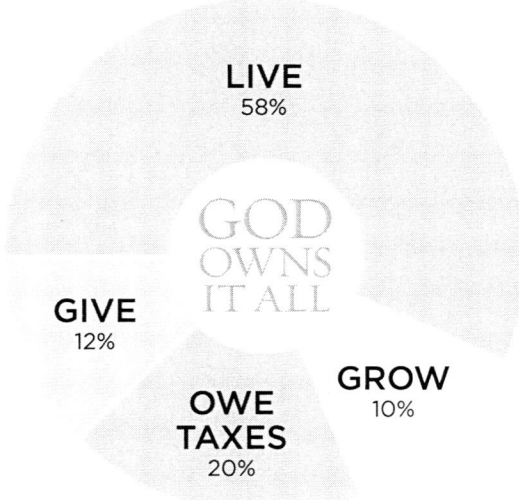

Do you see what happened? When you got rid of your debt and increased your giving by 8 percent, your taxes went down. This freed up even more money. With the extra money you were able to increase your lifestyle spending by 4 percent.

Go back and look at the pie diagram you completed in week 2 (p. 46). Now prayerfully ask God what He wants you to do. Is He calling you to pay off all your debt? Is He calling you to increase your giving? Is He calling you to save more? What is God telling you to do with His money? Now draw the pie that represents the financial picture God is showing you.

What needs to happen to make these priorities a reality?

Spend a few minutes in prayer, asking God to give you the conviction to begin taking the steps needed to implement the priorities represented by your pie diagram.

apply

After Judy and I had served in vocational ministry for a few years, it became clear that God was leading us to make a change. As we prayed about and discussed our options, we began applying many of the concepts and techniques I've presented in this Bible study. One of the primary tools we used was the decision-making process I shared this week.

After we had weighed all the considerations and alternatives, there were two clear paths we felt comfortable pursuing. One was to move back to Indianapolis near our friends and family and rejoin the CPA practice I had left, and the other was to remain in Atlanta and start a Christian financial-planning company. When we compared the two choices, moving back to Indianapolis was the clear winner. So that's what we did, right? Wrong.

We asked one additional question: What's the worst thing that could happen if we moved back to Indianapolis? The answer to that question was that we could fall back into the trap of living the country-club lifestyle we had left, and as a result, we could lose one of our kids to the trap of materialism. That risk was too great for us to take, so we stayed in Atlanta and started a financial-planning firm. That firm is now one of the largest fee-only registered investment advisers in the United States. More important, its clients have given away billions of dollars over the years.

When I started the financial-planning firm in Atlanta, we didn't have much, but we knew the principles you've been studying. The principles worked then, and they continue to work today. It doesn't matter what income tax bracket or life stage you're in. Simply apply biblical wisdom and then humbly follow God as you make the best decisions you can. The journey may be challenging, but I promise you that its rewards will far exceed your wildest dreams.

To end this study, I'd like to share my personal convictions about this week's topics. Then I want to give you an opportunity to review all your personal convictions and set some goals for your financial life.

Here are my personal convictions on this week's topics:

1. Savings is a tool we use to accomplish financial objectives. It isn't an end in itself.
2. We accumulate wealth by spending less than we earn over a long time period.
3. We can't accumulate enough to feel financially secure, significant, or successful.
4. "How much is enough?" differs for every family and is a number that should be determined prayerfully.
5. "How much is enough?" changes over time as circumstances change.
6. Net worth is always and only a measure of God's provision.
7. Goal setting is the beginning of meaningful life planning.
8. A goal isn't a goal until it's measurable.
9. Faith goals are critical for believers and the exclusive purview of believers.
10. A goal is always a statement of faith and is one of the primary ways we can see God's hand in our financial affairs.
11. A decision can never be any better than the best-known alternatives.
12. Decision making permeates every area of life.
13. Decision making is a process that, if followed, can eliminate much potential conflict.

**Record one or two personal convictions
from the topics we discussed this week.**

**In what ways do you feel encouraged
by what you learned this week?**

**How do you sense God moving you to change,
based on what you learned this week?**

Before we finish, it's important that you write down your financial goals. Studies have shown that people with written goals achieve a much higher success rate than those who don't write down their goals. Recording your goals also gives you the ability to remind yourself where you're going and to know when you're there.

Go back through all six weeks and review the personal convictions you recorded in the "Apply" section of your personal study each week. Ask God to show you what He wants you to do with your financial resources. Then write down up to five goals that God has put on your heart during this study. Copy them on a separate sheet of paper or on an index card and keep them in a visible place where they can remind you of your goals on a daily basis.

1. _____

2. _____

3. _____

4. _____

5. _____

6. _____

Even though you're completing this Bible study, perhaps you've never made the conscious decision to place your faith in Jesus Christ. If so, this decision is the most important thing you'll do in your whole life. Regardless of whether you ever get your financial house in order, please get your spiritual life in order. Read the following biblical truths about the salvation God offers you.

1. God loves you and has a wonderful plan for your life.
2. Every person is separated from God by sin—an innate propensity to follow self above all else.
3. Knowing that sin separates people from Him, God sent Jesus as the answer to the problem. As God's Son, Jesus came to bridge the gap between our sin and God's righteousness by becoming the sacrifice for our sin and by conquering death when He rose from the grave.
4. All people must choose whether to accept the truths of God's love, His plan for their lives, His power to overcome their sin, and Christ's sufficient payment for their sin. This choice is yours.

Read the following verses and ponder their meanings.

All have sinned and fall short of the glory of God.
Romans 3:23

The wages of sin is death, but the gift of God
is eternal life in Christ Jesus our Lord.
Romans 6:23

You are saved by grace through faith, and
this is not from yourselves; it is God's gift—
not from works, so that no one can boast.
Ephesians 2:8-9

Listen! I stand at the door and knock. If anyone hears
My voice and opens the door, I will come in to him
and have dinner with him, and he with Me.
Revelation 3:20

If you want to become a Christian, honestly tell God how you feel and use the following prayer as a guide to talk to Him: "God, I recognize that I'm a sinner, and I believe Christ is the answer. It's only His perfect life and death in my place that can save me from my sin. Because of Christ's sacrifice on the cross, I've been given His perfect record. I'm now completely loved and accepted by You, God. I give You full control over my life."

faith & finance

POWERED BY ORCHARD ALLIANCE

Introducing **FaithandFinance.org**, a new site to help you grow as an effective steward!

- *Thought-provoking* articles, videos, and resources
- *Biblically based* stewardship and generosity principles conveniently organized by life stage.

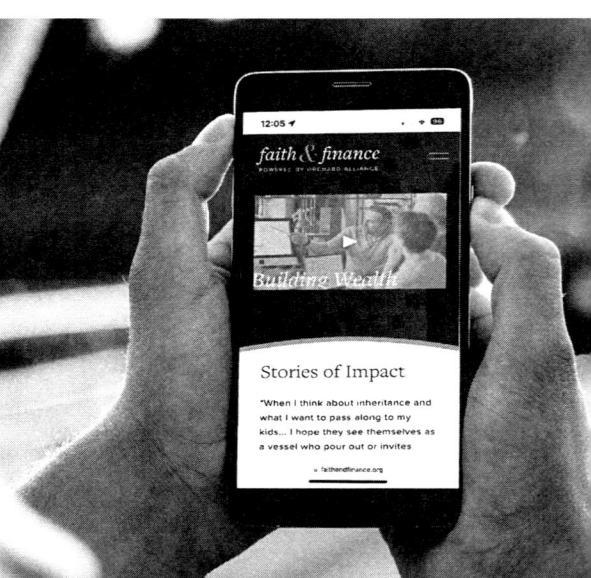